The Cheesecake Cook

Top 160 Most Delicious Cheesecake Recipes

Sharon Belcher

All rights reserved. No part of this book may be reproduced in any way or form without permission in writing from the author. No part of this publication may be reproduced or transmitted in any form or by any means , mechanic, electronic, photocopying, recording, by any storage or retrieval system or transmitted by email without the permission in writing from the author & publisher.

Contents

Zesty citrus cheesecake 8

Herry jell-o cheesecake 9

Classic cheesecake 10

Classic new york cheesecake 10

Chocolate cheesecake 11

No-bake chocolate cheesecake 12

Gluten-free diet cheesecake 12

Layered blackberry cheesecake 13

White chocolate raspberry cheesecake 14

Walnut crust cheesecake 15

Savoiardi cheesecake 16

Layered creamy orange cheesecake 16

Moist pecan cheesecake 17

Tropical pineapple cheesecake 18

Pumpkin cheesecake 19

Pineapple cheesecake 19

Peanut butter oreo cheesecake 20

Lemon raspberry cheesecake bars 21

Zesty cheesecake brownies 22

Caramel brownie cheesecake 23

Cheesecake-stuffed strawberries 24

Lemon & ginger cheesecake 25

Mini chocolate chip cheesecakes 27

Fruits of the forest cheesecake bars 28

Coffee cheesecakes 29

Peach melba cheesecake 31

Rum & raisin cheesecakes 33

Glazed fruit cheesecake 34

Champagne rhubarb cheesecake 36

Lemon meringue cheesecake	38
Mini baked blueberry cheesecakes	40
Key lime pie cheesecake	41
Tropical coconut cheesecake	43
Cheesecake charlotte	44
Vanilla cheesecake	46
Blueberry & lemon cheesecake	48
Raspberry ripple cheesecake	49
New york cheesecake	50
Plum crumble cheesecake	52
Caramelized banoffee cheesecake	54
Bananas foster cheesecake	55
Strawberry & cream cheesecake	58
Peanut brittle cheesecake	60
Honeycomb cheesecake	62
Chocolate hazelnut cheesecake	64
Brownie cheesecake	66
Toffee pudding cheesecake	67
Toffee pecan cheesecake	69
Peppermint bark cheesecake	71
Chocolate toffee cheesecake	73
Chocolate chilli cheesecake	74
Chocolate ginger cheesecake	76
Raspberry & pomegranate cheesecake	78
Salty honey cheesecake	80
Trifle cheesecakes	81
Alaska cheesecakes	82
Mini popcorn cheesecakes	85
Berry sundae cheesecakes	86
Valentine heart cheesecakes	88

Jelly & custard cheesecake	89
Macaron cheesecakes	91
Toasted marshmpermitcheesecake pie	94
Cheesecake pops	95
American pumpkin cheesecake	99
Florentine cheesecakes	101
Pine nut cheesecake	102
Crème brûlée cheesecakes	104
Rose & cardamom cheesecake	105
Crystallized flower cheesecakes	107
Profiterole cheesecake	109
Almond cheesecake	111
Cheesecake chocolates	113
Greek baklava cheesecake	115
Cardamom bun cheesecake	117
Polish cheesecake	119
Japanese cherry blossom cheesecake	120
Whisky & raspberry cranachan cheesecakes	122
Black forest cheesecake	124
Tiramisu cheesecake	126
Cheesecake tarts	128
Cheesecake lollipops	128
Toffee cheesecake bars	129
Bittersweet apple cheesecake roll	130
Cranberry cheese squares	131
Banana cheesecake	132
Chocolate truffle cheesecake	132
Chocomint cheesecake	133
Green tea mousse cheesecake	134
Frozen blueberry & lime cheesecake	134

Salted caramel ginger snap cheesecake 135
Coffee cheesecake 137
Chocolate melt cheesecake 137
Mint cheesecake 138
Toffee truffle cheesecake 139
Lime cheesecake 140
Chocolate snickers cheesecake 141
Double layer creamy pumpkin cheesecake 141
Caramel macchiato cheesecake 142
Vanilla mousse cheesecake 143
Red velvet cheesecake cups 144
Blueberry cheesecake cups 145
Honey cheese cups 145
Berry cheesecake cups 146
Mini berry cheese cups 147
Blackberry cheese cups 148
Chocolate cheesecake cups 148
Miniature cherry cheesecakes 149
Sundried tomato cheesecake 150
Roasted pepper pesto cheesecake 151
Feta cheesecake 152
Garlic mushroom cheesecake 153
Double cheese bacon cheesecake 154
Vanilla layered cheesecake 155
Raspberry cheesecake 155
Vanilla cinnamon cheesecake 156
Double berry cheesecake 157
Double-chocomalt cheesecake 158
Creamy lemon cheesecake 159
Melted marshmallow cheesecake 160

Caramel apple cheesecake 161

Butter-nutty cheesecake 161

Lemon berry cheesecake 162

Chocolate oreo cheesecake 163

Nutella cheesecake 164

Smoked salmon cheesecake 165

Ricotta asparagus cheesecake with swiss almond crust 166

Triple cheese & basil cheesecake 166

Creamy leek cheesecake 168

Pecan & olive cheesecake squares 168

Blue cheese & garlic cheesecake 169

Mexican cheesecake 170

Savory vegetable cheesecake 171

Chicken cranberry-orange cheesecake 172

Polenta pepper cheesecake 172

Blueberry cabernet cheesecake 173

Amaretto cheesecake 174

Double chocolate liqueur cheesecake 175

White chocolate frangelico cheesecake 176

Cheesecake icecream 177

Pecan liqueur cheesecake 177

Cointreau cheesecake 178

Coffee jelly cheesecake 179

Banana bourbon cheesecake 180

Rum-infused mousse cheesecake 181

White chocolate cheesecake 182

Margarita cheesecakes snacks 183

Vodka ricotta cheesecake 183

Rum praline cheesecake 184

Pina colada cheesecake 185

Tiramisu cheesecake 186

Rum & chocolate cheesecake 187

Vegan cheesecake 188

Tofu cheesecake 188

Cashew cheesecake 189

Strawberry cheesecake 190

Cashew lime cheesecake cups 191

Dulce de leche cheesecake bars 191

Lime cheesecake bars 192

Coffee cheesecake bars 194

One more thing 194

Zesty citrus cheesecake

Yield 8

What you need
1 egg yolk
1 tbsp lemon juice
1 tsp lemon zest, grated
1/4 tsp vanilla extract
1 1/4 c. All-purpose flour
1/3 c. White sugar
1/2 c. Butter
1 egg white
24oz cream cheese
1 2/3 c. White sugar
2 tbsp cornstarch
1 tbsp lemon juice
1 tbsp orange zest, grated
2 tsp lime zest, grated
1 1/2 tsp lemon zest, grated
1/2 tsp vanilla extract
3 eggs
1 c. Sour cream
2/3 c. Orange marmalade
2 tsp fresh lemon juice

What to do
Crust:
1. Heat up oven to 450 °f .
2. Beat egg yolk, 1 tbsp lemon juice, 1 tsp lemon peel & 1/4 tsp vanilla.
3. Mix flour & 1/3 c. Sugar with a food processor. Pour in butter & continue blending. Beat yolk mixture & blend till clumps form.
4. Press crust to the bottom of a lightly greased 9 in. Pan. Cool down for 10 min..
5. Brush crust lightly with egg white. Bake for 15 min..
6. Permit to cool on rack whereas preparing filling.

Filling:
1. Reduce oven temperature to 350 °f .
2. Mix cream cheese & 1 2/3 c. Sugar. Add cornstarch, 1 tbsp lemon juice, orange zest, lime zest, 1 1/2 tsp lemon zest & 1/2 tsp vanilla. Pour in eggs one at a time, next which mix in sour cream.
3. Pour mixture right into crust.
4. Bake for an hour. Turn off the oven, open the door & leave the cheesecake inside to cool next which refrigerate overnight.
5. Boil marmalade & 2 tsp lemon juice till slightly reduced for a couple of min. In saucepan.
6. Spread glaze on cheesecake. Permit to cool for a few min..

Herry jell-o cheesecake

Yield 8

What you need
2 1/2 c. Graham cracker crumbs
1/2 c. Butter, melted
6oz lemon flavored jell-o
1 c. Boiling water
8oz cream cheese
1 c. White sugar
1 tsp vanilla extract
3 tbsp lemon juice
12oz evaporated milk
21oz cherry pie filling

What to do
1. Blend together graham cracker crumbs & melted butter. Press 2 c. Of the mixture right into the bottom of a 9 in. Pan. Put to the side the remaining for garnish.
2. Dissolve lemon jell-o in boiling water. Put to the side.
3. Mix cream cheese, sugar & vanilla. Add jell-o mixture & lemon juice.
4. Whip evaporated milk in a separate bowl. Pour milk right into the cream cheese mixture & pour right into pan.

5. Permit to cool for a few hours. Add cherry pie filling & garnish with remaining crumb mixture.

Classic cheesecake

Yield 8

What you need
1 prepared graham cracker crust
16oz cream cheese
2 eggs
3/4 c. White sugar
2 tsp vanilla extract
1/2 tsp lemon zest, grated

What to do
1. Heat up oven to 350 °f.
2. Beat softened cream cheese slightly. Add eggs, sugar, vanilla, & lemon zest.
3. Bake for 30 min. & permit to cool afterwards before refrigerating for 8 hours.

Classic new york cheesecake

Yield 12

What you need
15 graham crackers, crushed
2 tbsp butter, melted
32oz cream cheese
1 1/2 c. White sugar
3/4 c. Milk
4 eggs

1 c. Sour cream
1 tbsp vanilla extract
1/4 c. All-purpose flour

What to do
1. Heat up oven to 350 °f .
2. Mix together graham crackers crumbs & butter. Press to the bottom of a lightly greased 9 in. Pan.
3. Blend cream cheese with sugar till you achieve a smooth texture. Add milk & mix it with eggs one at a time.
4. Pour in sour cream, vanilla & flour right into the mixture & blend till smooth. Pour filling right into mixture & bake for 1 hour.
5. Turn off the oven, open the door & leave the cheesecake inside to cool for 3-4 hours to prevent it from cracking. Let it cool in the fridge afterwards before serving.

Chocolate cheesecake

Yield 12

What you need
6oz cream cheese, softened
14oz condensed milk
1 egg
1 tsp vanilla extract
1 c. Chocolate chips
1 tsp flour
1 chocolate cookie pie crust

What to do
1. Heat up oven to 350 °f .
2. Mix cream cheese, condensed milk, egg & vanilla extract till smooth.
3. Cover chocolate chips with flour & pour right into the mixture.
4. Pour filling right into pie crust & bake for 35 min..
5. Refrigerate before serving.

No-bake chocolate cheesecake

Yield 10

What you need
8oz semi-sweet chocolate baking squares, melted & cooled
16oz cream cheese, softened
3/4 c. Brown sugar
1/4 c. Granulated sugar
2 tbsp milk
1 tsp vanilla extract
6oz chocolate crumb crusts
Sweetened whipped cream

What to do
1. Mix cream cheese, brown sugar, granulated sugar, milk & vanilla.
2. Pour in melted chocolate & continue beating.
3. Scoop right into crust & cool down inside fridge.
4. Garnish with whipped cream.

Gluten-free diet cheesecake

Yield 12

What you need
16oz low-fat cream cheese
3 eggs
1 c. Splenda
1 tsp vanilla
2 c. Sour cream
1/4 c. Splenda
1 tsp vanilla

What to do
1. Heat up oven to 350 °f .
2. Mix low-fat cream cheese, eggs, 1 c. Splenda & vanilla. Pour mixture right into a lightly greased 9 in. Pan.
3. Bake for 35 min..
4. Take away from oven & permit to cool.
5. Mix low-fat sour cream, 1/4 c. Splenda & vanilla. Pour over cheesecake & bake for 10 more min..
6. Refrigerate.

Layered blackberry cheesecake

Yield 8

What you need
3 tbsp butter, softened
1 c. Sour cream
1 c. Graham cracker crumbs
1/4 c. All-purpose flour
32oz cream cheese
1 tbsp vanilla extract
1 1/2 c. Sugar
1 1/2 pints blackberries
3/4 c. Milk
Zest & juice of 1 lemon
4 eggs

What to do
1. Heat up oven to 350 °f .
2. Mix graham cracker crumbs with 2 tbsp butter.
3. Press mixture to the bottom of a greased 9 in. Pan.
4. Whisk to mix cream cheese & sugar till smooth.
5. Blend in the milk & add eggs one at a time whereas mixing.
6. Add sour cream, flour & vanilla till smooth & divide the mixture evenly right into two bowls.
7. Purée blackberries, lemon zest & juice & pour right into one bowl of the mixture along with a half pint of blackberries & mix well.

8. Pour blackberry filling right into crust & bake for 10 min..
9. Take away pan from the oven & pour the remaining of the filling over the top.
10. Return the pan to bake for an hour till topping is set & cool down in the fridge till ready to serve.

White chocolate raspberry cheesecake

Yield 12

What you need
1 c. Chocolate cookie crumbs
3 tbsp white sugar
1/4 c. Butter, melted
10oz raspberries, frozen
2 tbsp white sugar
2 tsp cornstarch
1/2 c. Water
2 c. White chocolate chips
1/2 c. Half-and-half cream
24oz cream cheese, softened
1/2 c. White sugar
3 eggs
1 tsp vanilla extract

What to do
1. Heat up oven at 325 °f.
2. Blend cookie crumbs, 3 tbsp sugar & melted butter. Press to the bottom of a 9 in. Pan.
3. Mix raspberries, 2 tbsp sugar, cornstarch & water. Boil them in a saucepan & use a strainer to take away seeds afterwards.
4. Melt white chocolate in a pan of simmering water.
5. Blend cream cheese with half c. Sugar. Beat the eggs & pour them in one at a time. Pour in vanilla & melted white chocolate.
6. Pour half of the filling over the crust & add 3 tbsp of raspberry sauce on it. Pour the second half & do the raspberry sauce again on top.
7. Bake for an hour. Open the door & leave the cheesecake inside to cool & cool down in the fridge for 8 hours before serving.

Walnut crust cheesecake

Yield 12

What you need
Crust:
1 c. Graham cracker crumbs
1/4 c. Walnuts, finely chopped
3 tbsp brown sugar
1 tbsp ground cinnamon
1/2 tsp ground nutmeg
5 tbsp butter, melted

Filling:
24oz cream cheese
1 c. White sugar
1 c. Sour cream
1 c. Heavy cream
3 tbsp all-purpose flour
1 tbsp vanilla extract
3 eggs

What to do
Crust:
1. Heat up oven to 350 °f .
2. Mix graham cracker crumbs, walnuts, brown sugar, cinnamon, nutmeg & melted butter. Press to the bottom of a lightly greased 9 in. Pan.
3. Bake for 10 min. & permit to cool.

Filling:
1. Beat cream cheese & sugar till smooth.
2. Add sour cream, heavy cream & whereas still stirring.
3. Add flour & vanilla.
4. Add eggs one at a time.
5. Bake for an hour & cool down in the fridge overnight before serving.

Savoiardi cheesecake

Yield 12

What you need
9oz ladyfingers
19oz cream cheese, softened
1 tsp vanilla extract
1 c. White sugar
1 pint heavy whipping cream
21oz cherry pie filling

What to do
1. Arrange ladyfingers on the bottom of a 9 in. Pan.
2. Whip cream till smooth.
3. Mix together cream cheese, sugar & vanilla till smooth. Pour in the whipped cream.
4. Scoop 1/2 of cream cheese mixture right into pan.
5. Layer with ladyfingers & pour remaining cream cheese mixture over the top.
5. Finish with ladyfingers, topped off with the fruit pie filling. Refrigerate.

Layered creamy orange cheesecake

Yield 10

What you need
16oz cheese, softened
1/2 c. White sugar
2 eggs
3/4 c. Sour cream
1 tsp vanilla extract
1 tsp orange extract
2 drops yellow food coloring
1 drop red food coloring

Graham cracker crust

What to do
1. Heat up oven to 350 °f .
2. Mix cream cheese & sugar together till light & fluffy. Beat in eggs & mix well. Add sour cream & vanilla extract right into cream cheese mixture till smooth.
3. Pour a c. Of cream cheese mixture right into a small bowl & mix in orange extract, yellow food coloring, & red food coloring.
4. Pour plain colored mixture right into graham cracker crust. Drop orange batter over the top of the plain batter.
5. Bake for 30 to 35 min..
6. Turn off the oven, open the door & leave the cheesecake inside to cool & refrigerate.

Moist pecan cheesecake

Yield 8

What you need
1 1/2 c. Graham cracker crumbs
1/2 c. Pecans, chopped
1/3 c. White sugar
6 tbsp butter, softened
 Cream cheese, softened
2 c. White sugar
4 eggs, beaten
1 tbsp lemon juice
16oz sour cream
1/2 c. White sugar
1 tsp vanilla extract

What to do
1. Heat up oven to 325 °f .
2. Mix graham cracker crumbs, pecans, & 1/3 c. Of sugar in a bowl, & mix the softened butter right into the crumbs till mixed well.
3. Press to the bottom of a lightly greased 10-inch pan. Beat the cream cheese, 2 c. Of sugar, eggs, & lemon juice together. Spoon the batter on top of the crumbs.
3. Bake for 1 hour & 10 min.. Take away from oven & put to the side to cool.

4. Blend the sour cream, 1/2 c. Of sugar, & vanilla extract together. Pour sour cream mixture over cheesecake evenly.

5. Return to oven, & bake for 10 more min.. Refrigerate.

Tropical pineapple cheesecake

Yield 12

What you need
16oz cream cheese, softened
1 can sweetened condensed milk
1 c. Sugar
1 c. Coconut, finely flaked
1/4 c. Milk
1/4 c. Pecans, crushed
2 eggs
2 tsp vanilla extract
1 pinch salt
1 prepared graham cracker crust
8oz frozen whipped topping, thawed
15oz pineapple, crushed
3 tbsp coconut, finely flaked
1 tbsp pecans, crushed

What to do
1. Heat up oven to 350 °f .
2. Mix cream cheese, sweetened condensed milk, sweetener, 1 c. Coconut, milk, 1/4 c. Pecans, eggs, vanilla extract, & salt till smooth. Pour filling right into crust.
3. Bake for 35 to 40 min..
4. Cool down cheesecake in the fridge for 8 hours or more
5. Pour crushed pineapple evenly over cheesecake & top with whipped topping.
6. Garnish with 3 tbsp flaked coconut & 1 tbsp pecans.

Pumpkin cheesecake

Yield 10

What you need
16oz cream cheese
1/2 c. White sugar
1/2 tsp vanilla extract
2 eggs
1 prepared graham cracker crust
1/2 c. Pumpkin puree
1/2 tsp ground cinnamon
1 pinch ground cloves
1 pinch ground nutmeg
1/2 c. Frozen whipped topping, thawed

What to do
1. Heat up oven to 325 °f.
2. Mix cream cheese, sugar & vanilla. Mix till smooth. Add eggs one at a time. Take out 1 c. Of mixture & spread right into bottom of crust. Put to the side.
3. Pour pumpkin, cinnamon, cloves & nutmeg to the remaining mixture & mix lightly till well incorporated. Lightly pour the batter right into the crust.
4. Bake for 35 to 40 min..
5. Refrigerate for 3 hours or more.
6. Garnish with whipped topping.

Pineapple cheesecake

Yield 8

What you need
8oz cream cheese, softened
1/2 c. White sugar

30oz crushed pineapple, drained
1 3/4 c. Frozen whipped topping, thawed
1 prepared graham cracker crust

What to do
1. Beat together cream cheese & sugar. Add 1 can of pineapple & whipped topping & beat till smooth.
2. Pour mixture right into crust & top with remaining pineapple.
3. Refrigerate.

Peanut butter oreo cheesecake

Yield 12

What you need
4 1/2 c. Oreo cookies, crushed
1 c. Roasted peanuts, chopped
1/2 c. Butter, melted
32oz cream cheese, softened
5 eggs
1 1/2 c. Brown sugar
1 c. Peanut butter
1/2 c. Whipping cream
1 tsp vanilla extract
12 reese's peanut butter cups, broken right into small pieces

Topping:
3oz sour cream
1/2 c. Sugar

What to do
1. Heat up oven to 275 °f .
2. Blend crushed oreo cookies, peanuts & melted butter. Press to the bottom of a lightly greased 10 in. Pan.
3. Beat cream cheese. Add eggs one at a time. Add sugar, peanut butter & cream. Mix till well incorporated.
4. Add in vanilla next which add the peanut butter c. Pieces.

5. Pour batter over the crust. Put the 10 in. Pan right into a larger pan with 1 in. Water up the sides.
6. Bake for an hour & a half. Blend sour cream & sugar & spread evenly on the cheesecake.
7. Return to oven for 5 min.. Take away & permit to cool for an hour.
8. Cool down in the fridge before serving.

Lemon raspberry cheesecake bars

What you need
Crust:
30 vanilla wafer cookies
1/4 c. Butter, melted

Cheesecake:
1/3 c. Heavy cream
1/2 c. White chocolate
16oz cream cheese, softened
3/4 c. Granulated sugar
1 1/2 tsp cornstarch
1/2 c. Sour cream
1 tsp vanilla extract
2 eggs

Topping:
10oz lemon curd
48 raspberries

What to do
Crust:
1. Heat up oven to 350 °f .
2. Blend cookies in the food processor till it turns to fine crumbs.
3. Pour in melted butter & blend till mixed well.
4. Press to the bottom of a lightly greased baking dish.
5. Bake for 8 min. & permit to cool.

Filling:
1. Heat up oven to 300 °f.
2. Heat heavy cream in saucepan over low heat & mix in white chocolate. Mix continuously till melted. Put to the side.
3. Beat cream cheese, sugar & cornstarch till fluffy.
4. Add in sour cream, eggs & vanilla extract whereas slowly beating the whole mixture.
5. Pour filling right into crust & bake for 35 min..
6. Turn off the oven, open the door & leave the cheesecake inside to cool for 20 min..
7. Take away from oven & spread lemon curd on the cheesecake. Refrigerate for 3 hours.
8. Cut right into bars & finish with fresh raspberries.

Zesty cheesecake brownies

Yield 12

What you need
Brownies:
4oz unsalted butter, cut right into pieces
4oz unsweetened chocolate, chopped
1 1/2 c. Sugar
2 tsp vanilla extract
1/2 tsp baking powder
1/4 tsp salt
2 eggs
2/3 c. All-purpose flour

Cheesecake:
8oz cream cheese,
1/4 c. Sugar
1 egg
1 tsp grated orange zest
1 tbsp all-purpose flour

What to do
Brownies:
1. Heat up oven to 325 °f.

2. Mix butter & chocolate in a bowl & set over a pan of simmering water. Mix often till smooth. Take away bowl & permit to cool.

3. Mix sugar, vanilla, baking powder & salt right into the mixture. Add eggs one at a time. Lastly, add flour.

Cheesecake:
Combine cream cheese & sugar till smooth in a separate bowl for the cheesecake mixture. Add in egg, zest & flour.

Assemble:
1. Pour 1/2 c. Of brownie batter right into prepared pan.
2. Pour cream cheese mixture over brownie batter in pan.
3. Pour the remaining brownie batter in a swirl motion to create a marbling effect.
4. Bake for 45 min. & permit to cool afterwards.
5. Refrigerate. Cut right into squares.

Caramel brownie cheesecake

Yield 10

What you need
Brownies:
8oz butter, melted
1 c. Unsweetened cocoa powder
2 c. Granulated sugar
4 eggs
1 tsp vanilla extract
1 1/2 c. Flour
12oz hot fudge sauce

Cheesecake:
8oz cream cheese
1/2 can sweetened condensed milk
1 tsp vanilla

Topping:
4 full sized caramel biscuit bars

Caramel sauce

What to do
Brownies:
1. Heat up oven to 350 °f.
2. Mix cocoa & melted butter. Mix in sugar & add eggs one at a time. Add vanilla & keep stirring.
3. Add flour & hot fudge sauce.
4. Pour filling right into a lightly greased 9-inch pan & bake for 35 min.. Permit to cool & refrigerate.

Cheesecake:
1. For the cheesecake layer, mix cream cheese, sweetened condensed, milk & vanilla till smooth.
2. Spread mixture over brownies & top with twix bars. Refrigerate before serving.
3. Garnish with caramel sauce.

Cheesecake-stuffed strawberries

Yield 24

What you need
24 strawberries
12oz cream cheese
1 tsp vanilla
3 tbsp confectioners' sugar
1/2 c. Almonds, chopped fine in the blender

What to do
1. Pour cream cheese in a bowl & microwave for 30 min..
2. Blend cream cheese, vanilla & sugar till smooth.
3. Make a hole in the middle of each strawberry, but do not go all the way through the strawberry.
4. Scoop filling right into each strawberries.
5. Garnish with almonds.
6. Cool down strawberries in the fridge before serving.

LEMON & GINGER CHEESECAKE

For the crumb case

300 g/10½ ounces ginger biscuits/cookies

150 g/1¼ sticks butter, melted

For the topping

60 g/4 tbsp butter

Freshly squeezed juice & grated zest of 3 lemons

100 g/½ c. Caster/white sugar

3 big egg yolks

For the filling

6 sheets leaf gelatine

300 g/1⅓ c. Cream cheese

250 g/generous 1 c. Mascarpone cheese

100 g/½ c. Caster/white sugar

4 balls preserved stem ginger, finely chopped

60 ml/¼ c. Ginger syrup

250 ml/1 c. Double/heavy cream

A 23-cm/9-inch round springform cake pan, greased & lined

Serves 12

Start by preparing the lemon curd topping. Put the butter, lemon juice & sugar in a heatproof bowl set over a pan of simmering water. Whisk till the sugar has dissolved next which take away from the heat & put to the side to cool slightly. Whisk in the egg yolks & lemon zest, next which return the bowl to the pan over the water & mix all the time till the curd thickens. Leave to cool completely.

For the crumb case, crush the ginger biscuits/cookies to fine crumbs in a food processor or put in a clean plastic bag & bash with a rolling pin. Transfer the crumbs to a mixing bowl & mix in the melted butter. Press the buttery crumbs right into the base & sides of the prepared cake pan firmly utilizing the back of a spoon. You need the crumbs to come up about 3–4 cm/1½ in. High on the side of the pan so that they make a case for the filling.

To make the filling, soak the gelatine leaves in water till they are soft.

In a big mixing bowl, whisk together the cream cheese, mascarpone & sugar till light & creamy, next which beat in the chopped ginger pieces.

Put the ginger syrup & 120 ml/½ c. Water in a heatproof bowl set over a saucepan of simmering water & heat gently. Squeeze the water out of the gelatine leaves & add them to the warm ginger syrup, stirring till the gelatine has dissolved. Prudently add the ginger syrup to the cream cheese mixture, passing it through a sieve/strainer as you go to take away any undissolved gelatine pieces. Add the double/heavy cream & whisk everything together till the mixture is smooth & slightly thick.

Pour the filling right into the crumb case & tap it lightlyso that the mixture is even, next which cool down in the fridge for 3 hours or overnight.

Before serving, put spoonfuls of the lemon curd on top of the cheese filling & swirl them lightlyusing a knife to make pretty patterns.

MINI CHOCOLATE CHIP CHEESECAKES

For the crumb bases

100 g/3½ ounces oreo cookies

50 g/2 ounces pretzels

70 g/5 tbsp butter, melted

For the filling

250 g/generous 1 c. Cream cheese

250 g/generous 1 c. Ricotta

2 small eggs

1 tsp vanilla bean paste

200 g/scant 1 c. Condensed milk

200 g/1¼ c. Chocolate chunks

A 12-hole loose-based mini cheesecake pan/muffin pan, greased

Makes 12

Heat up the oven to 170°c gas 3.

    To make the bases, crush the oreos & pretzels to very fine crumbs in a food processor or put in a clean plastic bag & bash with a rolling pin. Transfer the crumbs to a mixing bowl & mix in the melted butter. Put a spoonful of the crumbs right into each hole of the prepared pan & press down firmly utilizing the end of a rolling pin or the back of a small spoon.

For the filling, whisk together the cream cheese & ricotta in a big mixing bowl. Add the eggs, vanilla bean paste & condensed milk & whisk again till smooth, next which mix in three quarters of the chocolate chips.

Pour the filling mixture right into the 12 holes of the pan leaving a little space in each hole as the cheesecakes will expand slightly during cooking. Bake in the preheated oven for 20–25 min. Till set with a slight wobble. Dash over the remaining chocolate chips straight away so that they melt slightly on the warm cheesecakes, next which leave to cool. When cool, take away from the pan & cool down in the fridge for 3 hours before serving.

FRUITS OF THE FOREST CHEESECAKE BARS

For the crumb bases

120 g/4 ounces digestive biscuits/graham crackers

70 g/5 tbsp butter, melted

For the filling

300 g/10½ ounces frozen fruits of the forest

75 g/scant ½ c. Caster/white sugar, or to taste

250 g/generous 1 c. Mascarpone cheese

250 ml/1 c. Crème fraîche

250 g/2 c. Berries , for the topping

A 12-cell silicone cake bar mould

Makes 12

Heat up the oven to 180°c gas 4.

To make the crumb bases, crush the biscuits/graham crackers to fine crumbs in a food processor or put in a clean plastic bag & bash with a rolling pin. Transfer the crumbs to a mixing bowl & mix in the melted butter. Press the buttery crumbs right into the base of each hole of the silicone mould firmly utilizing the back of a spoon, next which bake in the preheated oven for 10–12 min.. Leave to cool completely.

For the cheesecake filling, put the fruit & sugar in a saucepan with 60 ml/¼ c. Water & simmer till the mixture is thick & syrupy. Test the berries for sweetness & add a little extra sugar if you wish. Pass through a sieve/strainer to take away the seeds, next which leave to cool completely. Reserve a few spoonfuls of this fruit coulis to drizzle over the cheesecakes when serving.

In a big mixing bowl, whisk together the mascarpone & crème fraîche, next which fold in the remaining fruit coulis. Taste for sweetness & add a little more sugar if it is not sweet enough. Spoon over the crumb bases in the mould, next which transfer to the freezer. Leave till set, next which pop the bars of cheesecake out of the mould. Put on serving plates & leave to defrost. When you are ready to serve, arrange berries on top of each cheesecake & drizzle with the reserved coulis.

COFFEE CHEESECAKES

For the crumb bases

80 g/3 ounces amaretti biscuits/cookies

80 ml/⅓ c. Espresso coffee*, cooled

Coffee liqueur , to drizzle

For the filling

4 sheets leaf gelatine

200 g/scant 1 c. Cream cheese

200 g/scant 1 c. Mascarpone cheese

100 g/½ c. Caster/white sugar

160 ml/⅔ c. Double/heavy cream

80 ml/⅓ c. Espresso coffee*, cooled

1 tbsp coffee liqueur

To assemble

160 ml/⅔ c. Double/heavy cream

1 tbsp coffee liqueur

Cocoa powder, to dust

6 or 12 chocolate coffee beans

6 glasses or 12 espresso cups

Makes 6 or 12

*if you don't have an espresso machine, dissolve 1 tbsp coffee granules in 80 ml/⅓ c. Hot water, next which leave to cool before utilizing in the recipe.

For the bases, crush the amaretti biscuits/cookies right into small pieces with your hands or utilizing a rolling pin. Divide between the glasses or espresso c. & drizzle a little espresso & a little liqueur right into the base of each.

For the filling, soak the gelatine leaves in water till they are soft.

In a big mixing bowl, whisk together the cream cheese, mascarpone & sugar till light & creamy.

Put the cream & espresso in a heatproof bowl set over a pan of simmering water & heat gently. Squeeze the water out of the gelatine leaves, add them to the warm cream & mix till dissolved. Pass the coffee cream through a sieve/strainer to take away any undissolved gelatine pieces, next which whisk right into the cheese mixture along with the coffee liqueur. Spoon the cheesecake filling right into the glasses or espresso c. & leave to set in the fridge for 3 hours or overnight.

When you are ready to serve, whip the double/heavy cream & coffee liqueur together to stiff peaks. Spoon equally over the tops of the cheesecakes & dust with cocoa powder, finishing with a chocolate coffee bean.

PEACH MELBA CHEESECAKE

For the crumb case

300 g/10½ c. Malted milk biscuits/cookies

150 g/1¼ sticks butter, melted

125 g/1 c. Raspberries

For the filling

4 sheets leaf gelatine

4 ripe peaches, pitted

100 g/½ c. Caster/white sugar

200 g/scant 1 c. Cream cheese

250 g/generous 1 c. Ricotta

150 ml/⅔ c. Double/heavy cream

For the topping

1 packet glaze topping/fixing gel

Or

2 sheets leaf gelatine, freshly squeezed juice of 2 lemons & 30 g/

2½ tbsp caster/white sugar

3 ripe peaches

125 g/1 c. Raspberries

A 23-cm/9-inch round springform cake pan, greased & lined

Serves 12

To make the crumb case, crush the biscuits/cookies to fine crumbs in a food processor or put in a clean plastic bag & bash with a rolling pin. Transfer the crumbs to a mixing bowl & mix in the melted butter. Press the buttery crumbs right into the base & sides of the prepared cake pan firmly utilizing the back of a spoon. You need the crumbs to come up about 3–4 cm/1½ in. High on the side of the pan so that they make a case for the filling. Dash the raspberries over the base.

For the filling, soak the gelatine leaves in water till they are soft. Purée the peaches till smooth in a blender or food processor.

In a big mixing bowl, whisk together the sugar, cream cheese & ricotta till light & creamy.

Put the double/heavy cream in a heatproof bowl set over a pan of simmering water & heat the cream till it is only warm. Squeeze the water out of the gelatine leaves & add them to the warm cream, stirring till dissolved. Pass the cream through a sieve/strainer to take away any undissolved gelatine pieces, next which whisk right into the cheese mixture. Fold in the peach purée, next which pour the filling right into the crumb case & smooth level.

For the glaze, if utilizing a packet glaze, prepare according to the packet instructions. If making your own glaze, soak the gelatine leaves in water till softened. In a saucepan, lightlyheat the lemon juice & sugar with 250 ml/1 c. Water till the sugar has dissolved & the liquid is warm but not boiling. Squeeze the water from the gelatine leaves & add them to the pan, stirring till dissolved pass the glaze through a sieve/strainer, next which leave till only cool but not set.

Cut the peaches for the topping right into thin slices & arrange on top of the cheesecake. Dash over the raspberries & next which prudently pour over the cooled glaze. Leave to set in the fridge overnight.

RUM & RAISIN CHEESECAKES

For the filling

150 g/1 c. Mixed raisins

250 ml/1 c. Spiced rum

250 g/generous 1 c. Cream cheese

250 g/generous 1 c. Ricotta

2 small eggs

1 tbsp dark brown sugar

60 g/⅓ c. Caster/white sugar

For the crumb bases

150 g/5½ ounces chocolate digestive biscuits/graham crackers

75 g/5 tbsp butter, melted

For the rum sauce

100 g/7 tbsp butter

100 g/½ c. Caster/white sugar

160 ml/⅔ c. Double/heavy cream

A 12-hole loose-based cheesecake pan/muffin tin, greased

Makes 12

The day before you wish to make the cheesecakes, put the raisins & the rum in a bowl together, cover & leave to soak overnight.

Heat up the oven to 170°c gas 3.

To make the crumb bases, crush the chocolate biscuits/graham crackers to fine crumbs in a food processor or put in a clean plastic bag & bash with a rolling pin. Transfer the crumbs to a mixing bowl & mix in the melted butter. Put a spoonful of the crumbs right into each hole of the prepared cheesecake pan & press down firmly utilizing the end of a rolling pin or the back of a small spoon.

For the filling, whisk together the cream cheese & ricotta in a big mixing bowl. Add the eggs, sugars, half of the rum-soaked raisins & 2 tbsp of the soaking rum & whisk again till smooth. Spoon the mixture right into the 12 holes of the pan so that they are just about full. Bake the cheesecakes in the preheated oven for about 20–25 min. Till set with a slight wobble in the middle. Leave to cool, next which cool down in the fridge till you are ready to serve.

For the rum sauce, simmer the butter & sugar together in a saucepan till the sugar has dissolved. Add the cream & simmer for a few min.. Take away from the heat & mix in the remaining rum & raisins, next which put to the side to cool.

Serve the cheesecakes chilled with a small jug/pitcher of rum sauce on the side for drizzling.

GLAZED FRUIT CHEESECAKE

For the crumb base

200 g/7 ounces custard cream biscuits/cookies

100 g/7 tbsp butter, melted

For the filling

4 sheets leaf gelatine

200 g/scant 1 c. Cream cheese

250 g/generous 1 c. Quark/farmer cheese

100 g/½ c. Caster/white sugar

250 ml/1 c. Double/heavy cream

1 vanilla pod/bean

For the topping

Fresh fruit of your choice

1 packet glaze topping/fixing gel

Or

2 sheets leaf gelatine, freshly squeezed juice of 2 lemons & 30 g/

2½ tbsp caster/white sugar

A 23-cm/9-inch round springform cake pan, greased & lined

Serves 10

To make the crumb base, crush the custard creams to fine crumbs in a food processor or put in a clean plastic bag & bash with a rolling pin. Transfer the crumbs to a mixing bowl & mix in the melted butter. Press the buttery crumbs right into the base of the prepared cake pan firmly utilizing the back of a spoon.

For the filling, soak the gelatine leaves in water till they are soft.

In a big mixing bowl, whisk together the cream cheese, quark/farmer cheese & sugar till light & creamy.

Put the cream in a heatproof bowl. Split the vanilla pod/bean & take away the seeds with the back of a knife. Add the seeds & the pod to the cream & set the bowl over a pan of simmering water to heat gently. When warm, take away the pod/bean . Squeeze the water out of the gelatine leaves & add them to the warm vanilla cream, stirring till dissolved. Pass the cream through a sieve/strainer to take away any undissolved gelatine pieces, next which whisk right into the cheesecake mixture. Pour the mixture over the crumb base & cool down in the fridge for an hour.

For the topping, put the fruit in a pretty arrangement on top of the cheesecake. Prepare the glaze according to the packet instructions & pour over the cheesecake. If you are making your own glaze, soak the gelatine leaves in cold water. Heat the lemon juice in a saucepan with 250 ml/1 c. Water & the sugar till the sugar has dissolved & the mixture is warm but not boiling . Squeeze the water out of the gelatine leaves, add them to the pan & mix in till dissolved. Pass the glaze through a sieve/strainer, next which leave till only cool but not set. Pour the glaze over the fruit, next which leave the cheesecake to set in the fridge overnight before serving.

CHAMPAGNE RHUBARB CHEESECAKE

For the fruit

850 g/1 lb. 10 ounces pink champagne rhubarb

80 ml/⅓ c. Ginger syrup

50 g/¼ c. Caster/white sugar

For the crumb case

300 g/10½ ounces ginger biscuits/cookies

150 g/1¼ sticks butter, melted

For the filling

4 sheets leaf gelatine

200 g/scant 1 c. Cream cheese

250 g/generous 1 c. Quark/farmer cheese

30 g/2½ tbsp caster/white sugar

180 ml/¾ c. Double/heavy cream

For the topping

1 tbsp butter

1 tbsp golden/light corn syrup

30 g/generous 1 c. Cornflakes

A 23-cm/9-inch round springform cake pan, greased & lined

A silicone mat

Serves 10

Heat up the oven to 180°c gas 4.

Peel the rhubarb, cut it right into 7-cm/3-inch lengths & put in a roasting pan. Drizzle over the ginger syrup & dash with the sugar. Bake in the preheated oven for 15–20 min. Till the fruit is soft but still holds its shape. Take away from the oven & leave to cool. Purée half of the fruit in a food processor & reserve the remainder for the topping.

To make the crumb case, crush the biscuits/cookies to fine crumbs in a food processor or put in a clean plastic bag & bash with a rolling pin. Transfer the crumbs to a mixing bowl & mix in the melted butter. Press the buttery crumbs right into the base & sides of the prepared cake pan firmly utilizing the back of a spoon. You need the crumbs to come up about 3–4 cm/1½ in. High on the side of the pan so that they make a case for the filling.

For the filling, soak the gelatine leaves in water till they are soft.

In a big mixing bowl, whisk together the cream cheese, quark/farmer cheese & sugar till light & creamy, next which add the puréed rhubarb & fold it through.

Put the double/heavy cream in a heatproof bowl set over a pan of simmering water & heat gently. Squeeze the water out of the gelatine leaves & add them to the warmed cream, stirring till dissolved. Pass the cream through a sieve/strainer to take away any undissolved gelatine pieces, next which whisk right into the cheese mixture. Pour the mixture right into the crumb case & leave to set in the fridge for 3 hours or overnight.

For the topping, melt the butter & syrup together in a big saucepan, next which mix in the cornflakes, making sure that each flake is well covered. Spread the flakes out on a silicone mat or sheet of non-stick baking paper & leave to set.

When you are ready to serve, take away the cheesecake from the pan & put on a serving plate. Arrange the rhubarb pieces on top of the cheesecake & dash with the cornflakes .

LEMON MERINGUE CHEESECAKE

For the crumb case

300 g/10½ ounces digestive biscuits/graham crackers

150 g/1¼ sticks butter, melted

4 tbsp/¼ c. Lemon curd

For the filling

6 sheets leaf gelatine

300 g/1⅓ c. Cream cheese

250 g/generous 1 c. Ricotta

150 ml/⅔ c. Sour cream

100 g/½ c. Caster/white sugar

Freshly squeezed juice & grated zest of 2 lemons

For the meringue topping

150 g/¾ c. Caster/superfine sugar

60 ml/¼ c. Light corn syrup

3 egg whites

A 23-cm/9-inch round springform cake pan, greased & lined

A piping bag fitted with a big round nozzle/tip

A chef's blow torch

Serves 10

To make the crumb case, crush the biscuits/graham crackers to fine crumbs in a food processor or put in a clean plastic bag & bash with a rolling pin. Transfer the crumbs to a mixing bowl & mix in the melted butter. Press the buttery crumbs right into the base & sides of the prepared cake pan firmly utilizing the back of a spoon. You need the crumbs to come up about 3–4 cm/1½ in. High on the side of the pan so that they make a case for the filling. Spoon the lemon curd over the base of the crust & spread out lightlyinto an even layer with a spoon.

For the filling, soak the gelatine leaves in water till they are soft.

In a big mixing bowl, whisk together the cream cheese, ricotta, sour cream & sugar till light & creamy, next which mix in the lemon zest.

Put the lemon juice & 60 ml/¼ c. Water in a heatproof bowl set over a pan of simmering water & heat gently. Squeeze the water out of the gelatine leaves & add them to the warm lemon juice, stirring till the gelatine has dissolved. Pass the lemon jelly through a sieve/strainer to take away any undissolved gelatine pieces, next which add it to the cream cheese mixture & beat till it is smooth & slightly thick. Pour the filling right into the crumb case & cool down in the fridge for 3–4 hours or overnight till set.

For the meringue topping, heat the sugar, syrup & 4 tbsp water in a saucepan till the sugar has dissolved, next which bring to the boil. Whisk the egg whites with a balloon whisk or mixer till they form stiff peaks. Steadily pour the hot sugar syrup right into the egg whites in a thin stream & continue whisking till the meringue cools down & is glossy & firm. This will take about 10 min. & is therefore best done with a stand mixer.

Spoon the meringue right into the piping bag & pipe the meringue onto the cheesecake in high peaks. Lightly brown the meringue with a chef's blow torch or under a hot grill/broiler. Store in the fridge if you are not serving at once.

MINI BAKED BLUEBERRY CHEESECAKES

For the crumb bases

130 g/4½ ounces digestive biscuits/graham crackers

60 g/4 tbsp butter, melted

For the filling

250 g/generous 1 c. Mascarpone cheese

300 ml/1¼ c. Sour cream

2 eggs

70 g/⅓ c. Caster/white sugar

1 tsp vanilla bean paste

100 g/¾ c. Blueberries

6 small kilner jars or jam jars

Makes 6

Heat up the oven to 170°c gas 3.

To make the crumb bases, crush the biscuits/graham crackers to fine crumbs in a food processor or put in a clean plastic bag & bash with a rolling pin. Transfer the crumbs to a mixing bowl & mix in the melted butter. Divide the buttery crumbs between the jars & press down firmly with a spoon or the end of a rolling pin.

For the filling, whisk together the mascarpone cheese, sour cream, eggs, sugar & vanilla bean paste in a big mixing bowl till thick & creamy. Pour the filling prudently right into the jars, next which dash the blueberries evenly over the tops of the cheesecakes.

Place the jars in a big roasting pan half full with water, ensuring that the water is not so high as to spill out or go over the top of the cheesecake jars. Transfer the cheesecakes, in their waterbath, to the preheated oven & bake for about 25–30 min. Till only set but still with a slight wobble in the middle. Leave to cool, next which cool down in the fridge till you are ready to serve.

KEY LIME PIE CHEESECAKE

For the crumb case

300 g/10½ ounces digestive biscuits/graham crackers

150 g/1¼ sticks butter, melted

For the filling

6 limes

600 g/2⅔ c. Cream cheese

400 g/1¾ c. Condensed milk

For the candied lime zest

70 g/⅓ c. Caster/white sugar long grated zest of 4 of the limes

200 ml/¾ c. Double/heavy cream, whipped, for the topping

A 23-cm/9-inch round springform cake pan, greased & lined

A piping bag fitted with a big star nozzle/tip

Serves 10

Heat up the oven to 180°c gas 4.

To make the crumb case, crush the biscuits/graham crackers to fine crumbs in a food processor or put in a clean plastic bag & bash with a rolling pin. Transfer the crumbs to a mixing bowl & mix in the melted butter. Press the buttery crumbs right into the base & sides of the prepared cake pan firmly utilizing the back of a spoon. You need the crumbs to come up about 3 cm/1 inch high on the side of the pan so that they make a case for the filling. Bake the crumb case in the oven for 5–8 min., next which leave to cool completely.

For the candied lime zest, pare the zest of 4 of the limes right into long thin strips. Simmer the long strips of lime zest with the sugar & 60 ml/¼ c. Water for about 5 min. Till you have a thin syrup. Take away the lime zest from the pan & put on a wire rack to drain & cool.

For the filling, finely grate the zest of the 2 remaining limes, & juice all 6 limes.

In a big mixing bowl, whisk together the cream cheese, condensed milk, finely grated lime zest & the lime juice till smooth. Spoon the mixture right into the crumb case & cool down in the fridge for at least 3 hours till the cheesecake has set.

When you are ready to serve, spoon the whipped cream right into the piping bag & pipe big cream stars around the edge of the cheesecake. Decorate with the candied lime zest.

TROPICAL COCONUT CHEESECAKE

For the crumb case

300 g/10½ ounces coconut ring biscuits/cookies

150 g/1¼ sticks butter, melted

50 g/⅔ c. Long soft shredded coconut

For the filling

6 sheets leaf gelatine

300 g/1⅓ c. Cream cheese

250 g/generous 1 c. Mascarpone cheese

100 g/½ c. Vanilla sugar or 100 g/½ c. Caster/white sugar plus 1 tsp vanilla extract

400 ml/1¾ c. Coconut milk

250 ml/1 c. Double/heavy cream

1 tbsp coconut rum

For the topping

1 pineapple, peeled

60 ml/¼ c. Coconut rum

50 g/⅔ c. Coconut flakes

A 23-cm/9-inch round springform cake pan, greased & lined

A silicone mat

Serves 12

To make the crumb case, crush the coconut biscuits/cookies to fine crumbs in a food processor or put in a clean plastic bag & bash with a rolling pin. Transfer the crumbs to a mixing bowl & mix in the melted butter & shredded coconut. Press the mixture right into the base & sides of the prepared cake pan firmly with the back of a spoon. You need the crumbs to come up about 3–4 cm/1½ in. High on the side of the pan so that they make a case for the filling.

For the filling, soak the gelatine leaves in water till they are soft.

In a big mixing bowl, whisk together the cream cheese, mascarpone & vanilla sugar till light & creamy.

Put the coconut milk & double/heavy cream in a heatproof bowl set over a saucepan of simmering water & heat gently. Squeeze the water from the gelatine leaves & mix them right into the warm cream till the gelatine has dissolved. Pass through a sieve/strainer to take away any undissolved gelatine pieces, next which whisk the cream right into the cheese mixture along with the rum. Spoon the filling right into the crumb case & cool down in the fridge for 3–4 hours or overnight till set.

To make the pineapple topping, heat up the oven to 120°c gas ½. Slice the peeled pineapple very thinly & lay the slices on a silicone mat or sheet of baking parchment. Bake in the preheated oven for about 1½–2 hours till the pineapple is dried but not brown. Leave the pineapple to cool, next which put the slices in a shpermitdish & pour over the coconut rum. Cover & leave to soak for at least 1 hour.

Toast the coconut in a dry frying pan, stirring all the time to ensure that it does not burn, next which leave to cool.

When you are ready to serve, drain the pineapple of any excess liquid & arrange over the top of the cheesecake, leaving a border around the edge. Dash the toasted coconut flakes around the edge of the cheesecake & serve.

CHEESECAKE CHARLOTTE

For the crumb base

200 g/7 ounces digestive biscuits/graham crackers

100 g/7 tbsp butter, melted

For the filling

250 g/generous 1 c. Mascarpone cheese

300 ml/1¼ c. Crème fraîche

3 tbsp icing/confectioners' sugar

1 vanilla pod/bean, split

Finely grated zest of 1 lemon

For the strawberry sauce

300 g/2½–3 c. Strawberries

100 g/½ c. Caster/white sugar

To assemble

200 g/7 ounces savoiardi biscuits

200 g/1½–1⅔ c. Blueberries

200 g/1½–1⅔ c. Raspberries

400 g/3½–4 c. Strawberries

An 18-cm/7-inch round springform cake pan, greased & lined

Pretty ribbon, to decorate

Serves 8

To make the crumb base, crush the biscuits/graham crackers to fine crumbs in a food processor or put in a clean plastic bag & bash with a rolling pin. Transfer the crumbs to a mixing bowl & mix in the melted butter. Press the buttery crumbs right into the base of the prepared cake pan firmly utilizing the back of a spoon.

For the filling, whisk together the mascarpone cheese, crème fraîche, icing/confectioners' sugar, seeds scraped out of the vanilla pod/bean & lemon zest in a big mixing bowl till smooth. Spoon the mixture over the crumb base, level the top of the cheesecake & cool down in the fridge till set, preferably overnight.

Whilst the cheesecake is chilling, prepare the strawberry sauce by simmering the strawberries, sugar & the deseeded vanilla pod/bean in a saucepan with 80 ml/⅓ c. Water till the fruit is very soft & the liquid is syrupy. Pass the mixture through a sieve/strainer pressing out all the juice from the strawberries, next which discard the pressed fruit. Put to the side to cool.

When you are ready to serve, take away the cheesecake from the pan by sliding a round-bladed knife around the edge of the pan to release the cheesecake, next which put on a serving plate. Cut a quarter from one end of each sponge finger/ladyfinger so that that end is now flat rather than rounded, & arrange them upright & touching, in a standing ring around the sides of the cheesecake, with the rounded ends uppermost. The savoiardi should come up at least 3 cm/1 inch above the top of the cheesecake so that they create a wall to contain the fruit. Tie the ribbon tightly around the cheesecake to hold the savoiardi in place. Arrange the fruit on top of the cheesecake, next which use a pastry brush to brush a little of the strawberry sauce over the fruit to glaze. Serve with the remaining strawberry sauce to pour over the cheesecake.

VANILLA CHEESECAKE

For the crumb case

300 g/10½ ounces digestive biscuits/graham crackers

150 g/1¼ sticks butter, melted

For the filling

600 ml/2½ c. Crème fraîche

750 g/3⅓ c. Cream cheese

4 eggs

400 g/1¾ c. Condensed milk

2 tbsp plain/all-purpose flour, sifted

1 vanilla pod/bean

To serve

Fresh berries of your choice

Pouring cream

A 26-cm/10-inch round springform cake pan, greased & lined

Serves 12

Heat up the oven to 170°c gas 3.

To make the crumb case, crush the biscuits/graham crackers to fine crumbs in a food processor or put in a clean plastic bag & bash with a rolling pin. Transfer the crumbs to a mixing bowl & mix in the melted butter. Press the buttery crumbs right into the base & sides of the prepared cake pan firmly utilizing the back of a spoon. You need the crumbs to come up about 3–4 cm/1½ in. High on the side of the pan so that they make a case for the filling. Wrap the outside of the pan in cling film/plastic wrap & put in a roasting pan half full with water, ensuring that the water is not so high as to spill out. Put to the side.

For the filling, whisk together the crème fraîche, cream cheese, eggs, condensed milk & flour. Utilizing a sharp knife split the vanilla pod/bean in half, scrape out the seeds from both halves & add to the cheesecake mixture, discarding the pod/bean . Whisk till the seeds are evenly distributed, next which pour the mixture right into the crumb case. Transfer the cheesecake, in its waterbath, to the oven & bake for 1–1¼ hours till golden brown on top & still with a slight wobble in the middle. Take away the cheesecake from the waterbath & slide a knife around the edge of the pan to release the cheesecake & prevent it from cracking. Leave to cool, next which transfer to the fridge to cool down for at least 3 hours or preferably overnight. Serve with berries & pouring cream.

BLUEBERRY & LEMON CHEESECAKE

For the topping

350 g/2½–3 c. Blueberries

Freshly squeezed juice of 2 lemons

100 g/½ c. Caster/white sugar

For the crumb base

200 g/7 ounces digestive biscuits/graham crackers

100 g/7 tbsp butter, melted

For the filling

500 g/generous 2 c. Mascarpone cheese

500 ml/2 c. Crème fraîche

3 generous tbsp icing/confectioners' sugar, or to taste

Grated zest of 2 lemons

A 20-cm/8-inch square loose-based cake pan, greased & lined

Serves 10

Start by making the blueberry topping. Simmer the blueberries with the lemon juice & sugar in a saucepan for about 5 min. Till the fruit has burst & you have a thick sauce. Put to the side to cool.

To make the crumb base, crush the biscuits/graham crackers to fine crumbs in a food processor or put in a clean plastic bag & bash with a rolling pin. Transfer the crumbs to a mixing bowl & mix in the melted butter. Press the buttery crumbs right into the base of the prepared cake pan firmly utilizing the back of a spoon.

To make the filling, whisk together the mascarpone & crème fraîche in a big mixing bowl till smooth. Sift in the icing/confectioners' sugar, add the lemon zest, next which whisk again. Taste the mixture & add a little more icing/confectioners' sugar if you wish it to be sweeter.

Spoon the filling mixture over the crumb base & level with a knife or spatula, next which spoon the blueberry topping over the top. Cool down the cheesecake in the fridge for at least 3 hours or till set, next which cut right into slices to serve.

RASPBERRY RIPPLE CHEESECAKE

For the raspberry ripple sauce

125 g/1 c. Raspberries

100 g/½ c. Caster/white sugar

For the crumb base

150 g/5½ ounces digestive biscuits/graham crackers

90 g/6 tbsp butter, melted

125 g/1 c. Raspberries

For the filling

250 g/generous 1 c. Mascarpone cheese

250 ml/1 c. Crème fraîche

2 tbsp icing/confectioners' sugar, or to taste

1 tsp vanilla bean paste

An 18-cm/7-inch round loose-based cake pan, 5 cm/2 in. Deep, greased & lined

Serves 8

Start by preparing the ripple sauce as this needs to cool down before being swirled in the cheesecake. Simmer the raspberries & sugar with 60 ml/¼ c. Water for about 5 min. Till syrupy, next which pass through a fine mesh sieve/strainer to take away the seeds & put to the side to cool.

To make the crumb base, crush the biscuits/graham crackers to fine crumbs in a food processor or put in a clean plastic bag & bash with a rolling pin. Transfer the crumbs to a mixing bowl & mix in the melted butter. Press the buttery crumbs right into the base of the prepared cake pan firmly utilizing the back of a spoon. Arrange two thirds of the raspberries for the base in a ring around the edge of the pan, next which dash the remaining out over the middle of the base.

For the filling, whisk together the mascarpone & crème fraîche in a big mixing bowl till smooth, sift over the icing/confectioners' sugar, add the vanilla bean paste & whisk again. Taste for sweetness, adding a little more icing/confectioners' sugar if necessary.

Drizzle a little of the raspberry sauce over the raspberries on the base, next which pour half of the sauce right into the filling mixture & lightlyfold through till the mixture has thin ribbons of raspberry sauce running through it. Do not over mix or you will lose the pretty ripple effect.

Spoon the filling mixture over the crumb base. Put spoonfuls of the remaining raspberry sauce on top of the cheesecake a small distance apart, next which swirl them through the mixture utilizing a fork or a knife to make a pretty ripple pattern. Cool down in the fridge for at least 3 hours till the cheesecake has set.

NEW YORK CHEESECAKE

For the crumb base

150 g/5½ ounces digestive biscuits/graham crackers

90 g/6 tbsp butter, melted

For the filling

600 g/2⅔ c. Cream cheese

225 g/1 c. Clotted cream

100 ml/generous ⅓ c. Crème fraîche

140 g/¾ c. Caster/white sugar

4 eggs

1 tsp vanilla bean paste

For the topping

300 ml/1¼ c. Sour cream

3 tbsp icing/confectioners' sugar

A 26-cm/10-inch round springform cake pan, greased & lined

Serves 12

Heat up the oven to 170°c gas 3.

    To make the crumb base, crush the biscuits/graham crackers to fine crumbs in a food processor or put in a clean plastic bag & bash with a rolling pin. Transfer the crumbs to a mixing bowl & mix in the melted butter. Press the buttery crumbs right into the base of the prepared cake pan firmly utilizing the back of a spoon. Wrap the outside of the pan in cling film/plastic wrap & put in a roasting pan half full with water, ensuring that the water is not so high as to spill out. Put to the side.

For the filling, whisk together the cream cheese, clotted cream, crème fraîche, sugar, eggs & vanilla bean paste in a blender or with an electric whisk. Pour the mixture over the crumb base, next which transfer the cheesecake, in its waterbath, to the preheated oven & bake for 45–60 min. Till the cheesecake is set but still wobbles slightly. Take away the cheesecake from the oven & permitit to cool slightly so that the height of the cheesecake reduces. Leave the oven on.

To make the topping, whisk together the sour cream & icing/confectioners' sugar & pour over the top of the cheesecake. Return to the oven & bake for a further 10–15 min. Till set.

Take away the cheesecake from the waterbath & slide a knife around the edge of the pan to release the cheesecake & prevent it from cracking. Leave to cool completely in the pan, next which cool down in the fridge for at least 3 hours before serving.

PLUM CRUMBLE CHEESECAKE

For the topping

800 g/1¾ lbs. Red plums

50 g/¼ c. Caster/white sugar

2 tsp ground cinnamon

For the crumble

160 g/1½ sticks butter

200 g/1½ c. Self-raising flour

100 g/½ c. Granulated sugar

2 tsp ground cinnamon

For the filling

5 sheets leaf gelatine

300 g/1⅓ c. Cream cheese

250 g/generous 1 c. Ricotta

100 g/½ c. Caster/white sugar

250 ml/1 c. Double/heavy cream

A 23-cm/9-inch round springform cake pan, greased & lined

Serves 12

Start by preparing the plum topping. Heat up the oven to 180°c gas 4. Cut the plums in half & take away the stones/pits. Put the plums cut side down in a roasting pan. Dash with the sugar & cinnamon & add 100 ml/⅓ c. Water to the pan. Bake the plums in the preheated oven for 20–25 min. Or till soft, next which put to the side to cool. Reserve 12 baked plum halves & the baking juice from the pan for the topping & purée the remaining plums in a food processor.

Prepare the crumble by rubbing the butter right into the flour till the mixture resembles bread crumbs. Mix in the sugar & cinnamon & spread out over a big baking sheet. Bake for 10–15 min. Till the crumble is golden brown. Leave aside to cool next which break the crumble right into small pieces & dash two thirds of the crumble over the base of the prepared cake pan.

For the filling, soak the gelatine leaves in water till they are soft.

In a big mixing bowl, whisk together the cream cheese, ricotta & sugar till smooth.

Put the cream in a heatproof bowl set over a pan of simmering water & heat gently. Squeeze the water from the gelatine leaves & mix them right into the warm cream till the gelatine has dissolved. Prudently add the gelatine cream to the cream cheese mixture, passing it through a sieve/strainer as you go to take away any gelatine pieces that have not dissolved. Beat the mixture till it is smooth & slightly thick, next which mix in the plum purée. Pour the mixture over the crumble base & cool down in the fridge for 3–4 hours or overnight till set.

To serve, put the reserved 12 plum halves on top of the cheesecake & drizzle over the reserved plum juice. Dash the remaining crumble over the cheesecake to serve.

CARAMELIZED BANOFFEE CHEESECAKE

For the base

200 g/7 ounces digestive biscuits/graham crackers

50 g/¾ c. Dried banana chips

115 g/1 stick butter, melted

For the filling

2 ripe bananas

Freshly squeezed juice of 1 lemon

500 g/generous 2 c. Cream cheese

500 g/generous 2 c. Ricotta

4 eggs

1 tsp vanilla bean paste

400 g/1¾ c. Caramel condensed milk or dulce de leche

2 tsp ground cinnamon

For the topping

50 g/¼ c. Caster/white sugar

30 g/2 tbsp butter

4 ripe bananas, peeled & sliced freshly squeezed juice of ½ lemon

3 tbsp flaked/slivered almonds

A 23-cm/9-inch round springform cake pan, greased & lined

Serves 12

Heat up the oven to 170°c gas 3.

To make the crumb base, crush the biscuits/graham crackers & banana chips to fine crumbs in a food processor or put in a clean plastic bag & bash with a rolling pin. Transfer the crumbs to a mixing bowl & mix in the melted butter. Press the buttery banana crumbs right into the base of the prepared cake pan firmly utilizing the back of a spoon. Wrap the outside of the pan in cling film/plastic wrap & put in a roasting pan half full with water, ensuring that the water is not so high as to spill out. Put to the side.

For the filling, blitz the bananas & lemon juice to a smooth purée in a food processor, or mash together with a fork.

In a big mixing bowl, whisk together the cream cheese & ricotta. Add the eggs, vanilla, caramel condensed milk, cinnamon & banana purée & whisk again till smooth.

Pour the banana filling mixture over the crumb base, next which transfer the cheesecake, in its waterbath, to the preheated oven & bake for 1–1¼ hours till the cheesecake is set but still has a slight wobble in the middle. Take away the cheesecake from the waterbath & slide a knife around the edge of the pan to release the cheesecake & prevent it from cracking. Leave to cool completely in the pan, next which cool down in the fridge for at least 3 hours before serving.

Toast the almonds in a dry frying pan till golden brown, stirring all the time so that they do not burn. Transfer to a plate & leave to cool.

For the banana topping, heat the sugar & butter in a big frying pan till the sugar dissolves & caramelizes. Add the sliced bananas to the pan, tossing in the caramel till golden. Take away from the heat & squeeze over the lemon juice. Arrange the bananas on top of the cheesecake to serve & dash over the toasted almonds.

BANANAS FOSTER CHEESECAKE

For the base

2 small bananas

Freshly squeezed juice of ½ lemon

55 g/¼ c. Dark muscovado sugar

55 g/4 tbsp butter, softened

1 egg

75 g/generous ½ c. Self-raising flour

1 tsp ground cinnamon

30 g/¼ c. Walnut pieces

30 g/¼ c. Raisins

For the filling

4 sheets leaf gelatine

200 g/scant 1 c. Cream cheese

170 g/¾ c. Mascarpone cheese

100 g/½ c. Caster/white sugar

2 ripe bananas

Freshly squeezed juice of 1 lemon

250 ml/1 c. Double/heavy cream

2 tsp ground cinnamon

A few drops of yellow food colouring

For the rum sauce

100 g/7 tbsp butter

100 g/½ c. Caster/white sugar

1 tsp ground cinnamon

160 ml/⅔ c. Double/heavy cream

100 ml/generous ⅓ c. Dark rum

Grated white chocolate, to decorate

A 23-cm/9-inch round springform cake pan, greased & lined

Serves 10

Heat up the oven to 180°c gas 4.

To make the base, blitz the bananas & lemon juice to a smooth purée in a food processor, or mash together with a fork.

In a big mixing bowl, beat together the sugar & butter till light & creamy. Add the egg & beat again. Sift in the flour, next which add the banana purée, cinnamon, walnut pieces & raisins & whisk well so that everything is incorporated. Pour the mixture right into the prepared cake pan & bake in the preheated oven for 15–20 min. Till the cake is golden brown & springs back when pressed lightlyin the middle. Leave to cool in the pan.

For the filling, soak the gelatine leaves in water till they are soft.

In a big mixing bowl, whisk together the cream cheese, mascarpone & sugar till light & creamy.

Blitz the banana with the lemon juice to a purée in a food processor, or mash together with a fork, next which beat the purée right into the cheesecake mixture.

Put the cream & cinnamon in a heatproof bowl set over a pan of simmering water & heat gently. Squeeze the water from the gelatine leaves & mix them right into the cream till the gelatine has dissolved. Pass the cinnamon cream through a sieve/strainer to take away any undissolved gelatine pieces, next which whisk right into the cheese mixture. Add a few drops of yellow food colouring, & pour the cheesecake mixture over the cake base & tap the pan lightlyso that the cheesecake filling is level. Cool down in the fridge for 3 hours or overnight till set.

For the rum sauce, put the butter, sugar & cinnamon in a saucepan & simmer till the sugar has dissolved. Add the cream & simmer for a further few min.. Take away from the heat & mix in the rum, next which put to the side to cool.

Serve slices of the cheesecake drizzled with the rum sauce & dashd with the grated white chocolate.

STRAWBERRY & CREAM CHEESECAKE

For the base

55 g/4 tbsp butter, softened

55 g/¼ c. Caster/white sugar

1 big egg

55 g/½ c. Ground almonds

For the filling

200 g/2 c. Strawberries, hulled

225 g/1 c. Clotted cream

600 g/2⅔ c. Cream cheese

120 ml/½ c. Double/heavy cream

100 g/½ c. Caster/white sugar

4 eggs

For the topping

250 ml/1 c. Double/heavy cream, whipped to stiff peaks

200 g/2 c. Strawberries, halved

A 23-cm/9-inch round springform cake pan, greased & lined

Serves 12

Heat up the oven to 180°c gas 4.

For the base, cream together the butter & sugar in a big mixing bowl till light & creamy. Add the egg & whisk again. Fold in the ground almonds, next which spoon the mixture right into the prepared cake pan. Bake in the preheated oven for 10–15 min. Till golden brown, next which leave the base in the pan to cool.

When you are ready to prepare the filling, heat up the oven to 170°c gas 3. Wrap the outside of the pan in cling film/plastic wrap & put in a roasting pan half full with water, ensuring that the water is not so high as to spill out. Put to the side.

For the filling, blitz the strawberries, clotted cream, cream cheese, cream, sugar & eggs in a blender till smooth. Pour the strawberry cream over the sponge base, next which transfer the cheesecake, in its waterbath, to the preheated oven & bake for 50–60 min. Till the cheesecake is set but still wobbles slightly in the middle. Take away the cheesecake from the waterbath & slide a knife around the edge of the pan to release the cheesecake & prevent it from cracking. Leave to cool completely in the pan, next which cool down in the fridge for at least 3 hours before serving.

When you are ready to serve, take away the cheesecake from the pan & put on a serving plate. Spread the whipped cream over the top of the cheesecake, next which arrange the strawberries over the cream. Serve straight away or cool down in the fridge till ready to serve.

PEANUT BRITTLE CHEESECAKE

For the crumb base

250 g/9 ounces digestive biscuits/graham crackers

50 g/generous ⅓ c. Salted peanuts

100 g/7 tbsp butter, melted

For the filling

450 g/2 c. Quark/farmer cheese

600 g/2⅔ c. Cream cheese

250 ml/1 c. Double/heavy cream

4 eggs

100 g/½ c. Caster/white sugar

3 tbsp crunchy peanut butter

200 g/1¼ c. Milk chocolate chips

For the brittle

200 g/1 c. Caster/white sugar

80 ml/⅓ c. Golden/light corn syrup

150 g/1 generous c. Salted peanuts

2 tbsp crunchy peanut butter

1 tsp vanilla bean paste

50 g/3½ tbsp salted butter

1 scant tsp bicarbonate of soda/baking soda

For the topping

250 ml/1 c. Double/heavy cream

50 g/2 ounces dark chocolate, melted

A 23-cm/9-inch round springform cake pan, greased & lined

A sugar thermometer

A silicone mat or greased baking sheet

A piping bag fitted with a big star nozzle/tip

Serves 12

Heat up the oven to 170°c gas 3.

 To make the crumb base, crush the biscuits/graham crackers & peanuts to fine crumbs in a food processor or put in a clean plastic bag & bash with a rolling pin. Transfer the crumbs to a mixing bowl & mix in the melted butter. Press the buttery crumbs right into the base of the prepared cake pan firmly utilizing the back of a spoon. Wrap the outside of the pan in cling film/plastic wrap & put in a roasting pan half full with water, ensuring that the water is not so high as to spill out. Put to the side.

 For the filling, whisk together the quark, cream cheese, cream, eggs, sugar & peanut butter in a big mixing bowl till smooth. Mix in the chocolate chips & spoon the mixture over the base in the pan. Prudently transfer the cheesecake, in its waterbath, to the preheated oven & bake for 1–1¼ hours till the cheesecake is golden brown on top & still wobbles slightly in the middle. Leave to cool completely in the pan next which cool down in the fridge for 3 hours or overnight for best results.

 For the brittle, heat the sugar, syrup & 40 ml/3 tbsp water in a saucepan till the sugar has melted, next which bring to the boil till the temperature reaches 122°c or hard ball stage. Add the peanuts, peanut butter, vanilla paste & butter to the pan & beat well – the mixture will become stiff. Beat in the bicarbonate of soda/baking soda, next which tip the mixture onto the silicone mat or greased baking sheet, taking care as it will be very hot. Spread the mixture out right into a layer about 1cm/½ inch thick & leave to cool. When the brittle is cold, break it right into small pieces utilizing your hands or a rolling pin.

To assemble, take away the cheesecake from the pan. Whip the cream to stiff peaks next which spoon right into the piping bag. Pipe small stars in a ring around the outside edge of the cheesecake. Repeat with two more rings, leaving a gap in the middle. Dash over some of the peanut brittle and, utilizing a fork or spoon, drizzle with the melted chocolate in thin lines to decorate. Store in the fridge till you are ready to serve.

HONEYCOMB CHEESECAKE

For the honeycomb

200 g/1 c. Golden caster/natural raw cane sugar

3 tbsp runny honey

1 tsp vanilla bean paste

¼ tsp cream of tartar

30 g/2 tbsp butter

A pinch of salt

1 tsp bicarbonate of soda/baking soda

For the crumb base

200 g/7 ounces digestive biscuits/graham crackers

100 g/7 tbsp butter, melted

For the filling

600 g/2⅔ c. Cream cheese

300 ml/1¼ c. Sour cream

160 ml/⅔ c. Double/heavy cream

120 ml/½ c. Runny honey

4 eggs, plus 1 egg white

1 tsp vanilla bean paste

1 tbsp runny honey, to serve

A sugar thermometer

A silicone mat or greased baking sheet

A 23-cm/9-inch round springform cake pan, greased & lined

Serves 12

Start by preparing the honeycomb. Put the sugar, honey, vanilla, cream of tartar, butter, salt & 60 ml/¼ c. Water in a big heavy-based saucepan . Simmer till the sugar & butter dissolve, next which heat to 122°c , hard ball stage, taking care that the caramel does not burn. Take away the caramel from the heat & beat in the bicarbonate of soda/baking soda. Tip out straight away onto the silicone mat or baking sheet & leave to cool. When cool, break the honeycomb right into small pieces utilizing a rolling pin. Store half in an airtight container & keep the remainder out to add to the cheesecake.

Heat up the oven to 170°c gas 3.

To make the crumb base, crush the biscuits/graham crackers to fine crumbs in a food processor or put in a clean plastic bag & bash with a rolling pin. Transfer the crumbs to a mixing bowl & mix in the melted butter. Press the buttery crumbs right into the base of the prepared cake pan firmly utilizing the back of a spoon. Wrap the outside of the pan in cling film/plastic wrap & put in a roasting pan half full with water, ensuring that the water is not so high as to spill out. Put to the side.

For the filling, whisk together the cream cheese, sour cream, double/heavy cream, honey, whole eggs & vanilla in a big mixing bowl. In a separate bowl, whisk the egg white till foamy, next which mix in the honeycomb pieces & toss to cover them in the egg. Mix the honeycomb pieces right into the filling mixture , next which pour the mixture over the crumb base. Transfer the cheesecake, in its water bath, to the preheated oven. Bake for 45–60 min. Till the cheesecake is set but still wobbles slightly in the middle. The top will appear dark where the honeycomb has caramelized in the heat. Take away the cheesecake from the waterbath & leave to cool, next which cool down in the fridge for at least 3 hours.

When you are ready to serve, heat the honey lightlyin a saucepan, next which brush it over the top of the cheesecake with a pastry brush & dash with the reserved honeycomb.

CHOCOLATE HAZELNUT CHEESECAKE

For the crumb base

230 g/8 ounces hazelnut choc chip cookies

50 g/⅓ c. Plus 1 tbsp toasted hazelnut pieces

100 g/7 tbsp butter, melted

For the filling

6 sheets leaf gelatine

300 g/1⅓ c. Cream cheese

250 g/generous 1 c. Ricotta

200 g/generous ¾ c. Chocolate hazelnut spread, at room temperature

250 ml/1 c. Double/heavy cream

100 g/3½ ounces dark chocolate, chopped

10 ferrero rocher chocolates, quartered

For the topping

50 g/2 ounces dark chocolate, melted

3 generous tbsp chopped roasted hazelnuts

150 ml/⅔ c. Double/heavy cream, whipped

6 ferrero rocher chocolates

A 23-cm/9-inch round springform cake pan, greased & lined

A piping bag fitted with a big star nozzle/tip

Serves 12

For the crumb base, crush the cookies to fine crumbs in a food processor or put in a clean plastic bag & bash with a rolling pin. Transfer the crumbs to a mixing bowl & mix in the hazelnuts & melted butter. Press the buttery crumbs right into the base of the prepared cake pan firmly utilizing the back of a spoon.

For the filling, soak the gelatine leaves in water till they are soft.

In a big mixing bowl, whisk together the cream cheese, ricotta & chocolate hazelnut spread till light & creamy.

Put the cream in a heatproof bowl set over a pan of simmering water & heat gently. Squeeze the water from the gelatine leaves & mix them right into the warm cream till the gelatine has dissolved. Add the chocolate & mix till melted.

Prudently add the chocolate cream to the cream cheese mixture, passing it through a sieve/strainer to take away any undissolved gelatine pieces. Beat till the mixture is smooth & slightly thick, next which mix in the chopped ferrero rocher pieces. Pour the mixture over the crumb base & cool down in the fridge for 3–4 hours or overnight till set.

To serve, drizzle half of the melted chocolate in fine lines over the top of the cheesecake utilizing a fork. Dash the middle of the cheesecake with the hazelnuts & drizzle the remaining chocolate in fine lines over the nuts. Spoon the cream right into the piping bag & pipe 12 big stars of cream around the edge of the cheesecake. Cut each ferrero rocher in half utilizing a sharp knife & put one on top of each cream star. Store in the fridge till you are ready to serve.

BROWNIE CHEESECAKE

For the brownies

100 g/7 tbsp butter

150 g/5½ ounces dark chocolate

100 g/½ c. Caster/white sugar

100 g/½ c. Soft dark brown sugar

2 eggs

1 tsp vanilla extract

80 g/scant ⅔ c. Plain/all-purpose flour, sifted

50 g/½ c. Chopped pecans

For the topping

150 g/⅔ c. Cream cheese

160 ml/⅔ c. Sour cream

50 g/¼ c. Caster/white sugar

1 tsp vanilla bean paste

2 eggs

30 g/scant ¼ c. Plain/all-purpose flour, sifted

125 g/4½ ounces dark chocolate, chopped

A 23-cm/9-inch round springform cake pan, greased & lined

Serves 12

Heat up the oven to 180°c gas 4.

To prepare the brownies, melt the butter & chocolate in a heatproof bowl set over a small pan of simmering water, taking care that the bottom of the bowl does not touch the water. Mix till melted, next which leave to cool.

In a big mixing bowl, whisk together the sugars & eggs with the vanilla till doubled in size & the mixture is very light & creamy. Slowly pour in the cooled melted chocolate mixture, whisking all the time. Fold in the flour & nuts, next which pour right into the prepared cake pan.

For the cheesecake topping, whisk together the cream cheese, sour cream, sugar, vanilla, eggs & flour till smooth, next which mix through the chopped chocolate. Put big spoonfuls of the cheesecake mixture at intervals on top of the brownie mixture. Swirl the cheesecake & brownie mixtures together with a round-bladed knife to create swirled patterns.

Bake the cheesecake in the preheated oven for 40–45 min. Till a crust has formed on the brownie & the cheesecake mixture is set. Permitto cool before serving.

TOFFEE PUDDING CHEESECAKE

For the cake base

60 g/4 tbsp butter, softened

60 g/⅓ c. Muscovado sugar

1 egg

60 g/scant ½ c. Self-raising flour

1 generous tbsp crème fraîche

40 g/⅓ c. Finely chopped pecan nuts

40 g/¼ c. Finely chopped dates

For the filling

600 ml/2½ c. Crème fraîche

600 g/2⅔ c. Cream cheese

4 eggs

400 g/1¾ c. Caramel condensed milk or dulce de leche

For the toffee sauce

80 g/scant ½ c. Caster/white sugar

40 g/3¼ tbsp muscovado sugar

50 g/3½ tbsp butter

A pinch of salt

250 ml/1 c. Double/heavy cream

Clotted cream or crème fraîche, to serve

A 23-cm/9-inch round springform cake pan, greased & lined

Serves 12

Heat up the oven to 180°c gas 4.

For the base, whisk together the butter & sugar in a big mixing bowl till creamy. Add the egg & beat again. Sift in the flour & add the crème fraîche, pecan nuts & dates. Spoon the mixture right into the prepared cake pan & bake for 15–20 min. Till the cake is golden brown & springs back when pressed lightlyin the middle. Leave to cool in the pan. Turn the oven temperature down to 170°c gas 3.

When the base is cool, wrap the outside of the pan in cling film/plastic wrap & put in a roasting pan half full with water, ensuring that the water is not so high as to spill out. Put to the side.

For the filling, whisk together the crème fraîche, cream cheese, eggs & caramel condensed milk. Pour the mixture on top of the cake base & transfer the cheesecake, in its waterbath, to the preheated oven. Bake for 1–1¼ hours till golden brown on top & still with a slight wobble in the middle. Take away the cheesecake from the waterbath & slide a knife around the edge of the pan to release the cheesecake & prevent it from cracking. Leave to cool, next which transfer to the fridge to cool down for at least 3 hours or preferably overnight.

For the toffee sauce, put the sugars, butter, salt & 200 ml/¾ c. Of the cream in a heavy-based saucepan set over a gentle heat & simmer till the sugar has dissolved & you have a thick toffee sauce. Take away from the heat & add the remaining 50 ml/¼ c. Cream. Leave to cool next which serve with the cheesecake, along with clotted cream or crème fraîche.

TOFFEE PECAN CHEESECAKE

For the nut crust

30 g/2 tbsp butter, softened

100 g/1 c. Finely chopped pecans

For the filling

600 g/2⅔ c. Cream cheese

500 g/generous 2 c. Ricotta

4 big eggs

250 ml/1 c. Maple syrup

For the topping

75 g/generous ⅓ c. Caster/white sugar

75 g/packed ⅓ c. Dark brown sugar

3 tbsp golden/light corn syrup

1 generous tsp ground cinnamon

1 tsp vanilla bean paste

40 g/3 tbsp butter

1 egg, plus 1 egg yolk, beaten

100 g/generous ¾ c. Pecan halves

A 26-cm/10-inch round springform cake pan, greased & lined

Serves 12

Heat up the oven to 170°c gas 3.

    To prepare the pan, spread the softened butter around the sides & base of the pan. Dash the chopped pecan nuts right into the pan & shake the pan so that the base & sides are covered with pecan pieces.

In a big mixing bowl, whisk together the cream cheese & ricotta, next which add the eggs & maple syrup & whisk till the mixture is smooth. Spoon the mixture right into the prepared pan, set the pan on a big baking sheet & bake in the preheated oven for 45–60 min.. The cheesecake is cooked when it is golden brown on top & the middle still has a very slight wobble. Slide a knife around the edge of the pan to release the cheesecake & prevent it from cracking, next which leave to cool.

To prepare the caramel glaze for the topping, heat the sugars, syrup, cinnamon, vanilla paste & butter in a saucepan till the sugars have dissolved & the mixture is syrupy. Take away from the heat & let cool for 10 min., next which whisk in the beaten egg & yolk. Pass the mixture through a sieve/strainer to take away any impurities.

Arrange the pecan halves in a ring around the edge of the cheesecake whilst still in the pan, next which spoon over some of the caramel glaze. You may not need all of the glaze but any extra can be served alongside the cheesecake to drizzle over. Cool down the cheesecake in the fridge overnight for best results & take away from the pan only before serving.

PEPPERMINT BARK CHEESECAKE

For the crumb base

180 g/6 ounces chocolate oat biscuits/cookies

60 g/4 tbsp butter, melted

For the filling

100 g/3½ ounces white chocolate

250 g/generous 1 c. Mascarpone cheese

250 ml/1 c. Crème fraîche

1 tsp peppermint extract

1 tsp vanilla extract

For the peppermint bark

150 g/5½ ounces white chocolate

1 tsp peppermint extract

5 peppermint candy canes

White edible glitter

A 20-cm/8-inch loose-based cake pan, greased & lined

A silicone mat

Serves 10

To make the base, crush the biscuits/cookies to fine crumbs in a food processor or put in a clean plastic bag & bash with a rolling pin. Transfer the crumbs to a mixing bowl & mix in the melted butter. Press the buttery crumbs right into the base of the prepared cake pan firmly utilizing the back of a spoon.

For the filling, melt the white chocolate in a heatproof bowl set over a pan of simmering water. Take away the bowl from the heat & leave the chocolate to cool, but not set.

In a big mixing bowl, whisk together the mascarpone & crème fraîche in a big mixing bowl. Mix through the cooled white chocolate & the peppermint & vanilla extracts. It is important that the white chocolate is cool when it is added to the mixture otherwise it will set in small pieces in the cream. Spoon the mixture over the crumb base & level with a spatula. Cool down in the fridge for at least 3 hours.

For the peppermint bark, melt the chocolate in a heatproof bowl set over a pan of simmering water. Take away from the heat & mix in the peppermint extract, next which spread out in a thin layer on a silicone mat or sheet of greaseproof/waxed paper. Crush the peppermint candy canes right into small pieces in a clean plastic bag utilizing a rolling pin, next which dash the red & white candy pieces over the white chocolate & leave to set in the fridge.

When ready to serve, take away the cheesecake from the pan & put it on a serving plate. Break the peppermint bark right into small shards utilizing a sharp knife & decorate the top of the cheesecake with them. Dash with edible glitter, if using, to serve.

CHOCOLATE TOFFEE CHEESECAKE

For the crumb base

250 g/9 ounces caramelized biscuits/cookies

125 g/1 stick plus 1 tbsp butter, melted

For the filling

400 g/1¾ c. Cream cheese

250 g/generous 1 c. Ricotta

225 g/1 c. Clotted cream

400 g/1¾ c. Condensed milk

Finely grated zest of 1 lemon

4 eggs

180 g/6 ounces chopped daim/heath bar

A 23-cm/9-inch round springform cake pan, greased & lined

Serves 12

Heat up the oven to 170°c gas 3.

To make the crumb base, crush the biscuits/cookies to fine crumbs in a food processor or put in a clean plastic bag & bash with a rolling pin. Transfer the crumbs to a mixing bowl & mix in the melted butter. Press the buttery crumbs right into the base of the prepared cake pan firmly utilizing the back of a spoon.

For the filling, whisk together the cream cheese, ricotta & clotted cream in a big mixing bowl. Add the condensed milk, lemon zest & eggs & whisk again till smooth. Mix in two thirds of the daim/heath bars so that they are evenly distributed, next which pour the mixture over the crumb base.

Bake the cheesecake in the preheated oven for 10 min., next which prudently dash the remaining chopped daim/heath bars over the top of the cheesecake. A slight skin will have formed on top of the cheesecake which will hold the daim/heath bar pieces on top of the cheesecake. Bake for a further 40–50 min. Till the cheesecake is set but still wobbles slightly in the middle. Leave to cool completely next which cool down for at least 3 hours in the fridge before serving.

CHOCOLATE CHILLI CHEESECAKE

For the decoration

8 bird's eye chillies

100 g/½ c. Caster/white sugar

For the crumb base

250 g/9 ounces chocolate digestive biscuits/graham crackers

100 g/7 tbsp butter, melted

For the filling

6 sheets leaf gelatine

300 g/1⅓ c. Cream cheese

250 g/generous 1 c. Mascarpone cheese

100 g/½ c. Caster/white sugar

400 ml/1¾ c. Double/heavy cream

100 g/3½ ounces dark chilli chocolate, melted

For the topping

100 g/3½ ounces dark chilli chocolate

60 ml/¼ c. Double/heavy cream

20 g/1½ tbsp butter

60 ml/¼ c. Golden/light corn syrup

8 x 6-cm/2½-inch diameter chef's rings , greased

Makes 8

Start by preparing the chillies. Put them in a saucepan with the sugar & 250 ml/1 c. Water & simmer for 15 min. Till the chillies are soft & the liquid is syrupy. Put to the side to cool in the syrup.

To make the crumb bases, crush the biscuits/graham crackers to fine crumbs in a food processor or put in a clean plastic bag & bash with a rolling pin. Transfer the crumbs to a mixing bowl & mix in the melted butter. Put the chef's rings on a baking sheet & divide the buttery crumbs between them, pressing down firmly with the back of a spoon.

For the filling, soak the gelatine leaves in water till they are soft.

In a big mixing bowl, whisk together the cream cheese, mascarpone & sugar till light & creamy.

Put the cream in a heatproof bowl set over a saucepan of simmering water, & heat gently. Squeeze the water out of the gelatine leaves & mix them right into the warm cream till the gelatine has dissolved. Pass through a sieve/strainer to take away any undissolved gelatine pieces, next which mix in the melted chilli chocolate. Prudently add the chocolate cream to the cream cheese mixture & beat till everything is incorporated. Pour the mixture over the crumb bases in the chef's rings.

For the ganache topping, put the chocolate, cream & butter in a heatproof bowl set over a pan of simmering water & mix till the chocolate & butter have melted. Add the syrup & mix again till glossy. Take away from the heat & leave to cool for a few min. Next which lightlyspread over the top of the cheesecakes. Cool down in the fridge for 3 hours or overnight till the cheesecakes are set. To serve, take away the cheesecakes from the chef's rings & top each with a candied chilli .

CHOCOLATE GINGER CHEESECAKE

For the crumb case

300 g/10½ ounces ginger biscuits/cookies

150 g/1¼ sticks butter, melted

For the filling

650 g/2¾–3 c. Cream cheese

600 ml/2½ c. Crème fraîche

4 eggs

100 g/½ c. Caster/white sugar

200 g/7 ounces dark chocolate, melted & cooled

6 balls preserved stem ginger, finely chopped

1 tbsp ginger syrup

150 g/5½ ounces dark chocolate, chopped

2 tbsp plain/all-purpose flour, sifted

For the topping

150 g/5½ ounces white chocolate

30 g/1 ounces dark chocolate

A 23-cm/9-inch round springform cake pan, greased & lined

A piping bag fitted with a small round nozzle/tip

Serves 12

Heat up the oven to 170°c gas 3.

To make the crumb case, crush the biscuits/cookies to fine crumbs in a food processor or put in a clean plastic bag & bash with a rolling pin. Transfer the crumbs to a mixing bowl & mix in the melted butter. Press the buttery crumbs right into the base & sides of the prepared cake pan firmly utilizing the back of a spoon. You need the crumbs to come up about 3–4 cm/1½ in. High on the side of the pan so that they make a case for the filling. Wrap the outside of the pan in cling film/plastic wrap & put in a roasting pan half full with water, ensuring that the water is not so high as to spill out. Put to the side.

For the filling, whisk together the cream cheese, crème fraîche, eggs, sugar, melted chocolate, finely chopped ginger, syrup & chopped chocolate in a big mixing bowl. Sift the flour over the mixture & mix in, next which pour the mixture right into the crumb case. Bake in the preheated oven for 1–1¼ hours till set but still with a slight wobble in the middle. Turn off the heat & leave to cool completely in the oven, next which transfer to the fridge to cool down for at least 3 hours or preferably overnight.

Once chilled, melt the white & dark chocolate for the decoration in separate heatproof bowls set over 2 pans of simmering water. Leave to cool slightly, next which spread the white chocolate in a thin layer over the top of the cheesecake. Spoon the dark chocolate right into the piping bag & pipe swirls over the top of the cheesecake in pretty patterns. If you do not have a piping bag, you can swirl patterns of the chocolate utilizing a spoon. Cool down in the fridge till the chocolate has set before serving.

RASPBERRY & POMEGRANATE CHEESECAKE

For the crumb base

200 g/7 ounces digestive biscuits/graham crackers

100 g/7 tbsp butter, melted

150 g/generous 1 c. Raspberries

50 g/⅓ c. White chocolate chips

For the filling

6 sheets leaf gelatine

300 g/1⅓ c. Cream cheese

250 g/generous 1 c. Ricotta

100 g/½ c. Caster/white sugar

150 ml/⅔ c. Sour cream

100 ml/generous ⅓ c. Hibiscus syrup

2 tbsp rose liqueur or syrup

For the topping

80 g/scant ½ c. Caster/white sugar

12 hibiscus flowers

Pomegranate seeds

A 23-cm/9-inch round springform cake pan, greased & lined

A silicone mat

Serves 12

For the base, crush the biscuits/graham crackers to fine crumbs in a food processor or put in a clean plastic bag & bash with a rolling pin. Transfer the crumbs to a mixing bowl & mix in the melted butter. Press the buttery crumbs right into the base of the prepared cake pan firmly utilizing the back of a spoon. Dash the raspberries & chocolate chips over the base of the cheesecake.

For the filling, soak the gelatine leaves in water till they are soft.

In a big mixing bowl, whisk together the cream cheese, ricotta, sugar & sour cream till light & creamy.

Put the hibiscus syrup & rose liqueur in a heatproof bowl resting over a pan of simmering water & heat gently. Squeeze the water from the gelatine leaves & mix them right into the warm syrup till the gelatine has dissolved. Prudently add the gelatine liquid to the cream cheese mixture, passing it through a sieve/strainer to take away any gelatine pieces that have not dissolved. Beat till the mixture is smooth & slightly thick, next which pour over the base & cool down in the fridge for 3–4 hours or overnight till set.

For the topping, put the sugar in a heavy-based saucepan & heat till the sugar melts & starts to caramelize. Do not stir, but lightlyswirl the caramel by shaking the pan. When the caramel is golden brown, take away from the heat & leave to stand for a min. Or so till the caramel only starts to thicken. Utilizing a fork drizzle spirals & zigzags of the caramel onto the silicone mat or a sheet of greaseproof/waxed paper to make pretty decorations. Leave to cool, next which store in an airtight container till needed. The caramel will become sticky if exposed to the air, so it is best to make these only an hour or so before you wish to serve the cheesecake.

When you are ready to serve, arrange the hibiscus flowers in a ring on top of the cheesecake & dash over the pomegranate seeds. Decorate with the sugar decorations & serve straight away

SALTY HONEY CHEESECAKE

For the crumb base

250 g/9 ounces caramelized biscuits/cookies

125 g/1 stick plus 1 tbsp butter, melted

For the cheesecake

125 g/1 stick plus 1 tbsp butter, melted

170 g/generous ¾ c. Caster/white sugar

½ tsp sea salt flakes

300 g/1 c. Honey

1 tsp vanilla bean paste

2 tsp white wine vinegar

300 g/1⅓ c. Cream cheese

250 ml/1 c. Double/heavy cream

4 eggs

A 23-cm/9-inch round springform cake pan, greased & lined

Serves 12

Heat up the oven to 170°c gas 3.

To make the crumb base, crush the caramelized biscuits/cookies to fine crumbs in a food processor or put in a clean plastic bag & bash with a rolling pin. Transfer the crumbs to a mixing bowl & mix in the melted butter. Press the buttery crumbs right into the base of the prepared cake pan firmly utilizing the back of a spoon.

For the filling, whisk together the melted butter, sugar, salt flakes, honey, vanilla, vinegar & cream cheese in a big mixing bowl till smooth. Add the cream, next which beat in the eggs one at a time, whisking between each addition. Pour the mixture over the crumb base & bake in the preheated oven for 45 min.. Reduce the oven temperature to 150°c gas 2 & bake for about 15 min. More till the cheesecake is set but still has a slight wobble in the middle. Turn off the heat & leave the cheesecake to cool completely in the oven, next which transfer to the fridge to cool down for at least 3 hours or overnight before serving.

TRIFLE CHEESECAKES

1 small raspberry jam swiss roll/jelly roll

200 g/1½ c. Fresh raspberries

3 generous tbsp amaretto or almond liqueur

65 g/2½ ounces raspberry jelly cubes/jello powder

250 g/generous 1 c. Mascarpone cheese

250 ml/1 c. Sour cream

2 tbsp icing/confectioners' sugar, or to taste

1 tsp vanilla bean paste

Sugar dashs, to decorate

6 small kilner jars or jam jars with lids

A piping bag fitted with a big round nozzle/tip

Serves 6

Cut the swiss roll/jelly roll right into thin slices, next which cut each slice in half. Arrange the slices around the sides of each jar & a slice in the base. Dash over the raspberries & drizzle with the amaretto.

Make up the raspberry jelly/jello according to the package instructions & pour it right into the jars, dividing it equally between them. Leave to set in the fridge.

Once the jelly/jello has set, prepare the cheesecake topping. In a big mixing bowl, whisk together the mascarpone & sour cream till smooth. Sift the icing/confectioners' sugar over the mixture, add the vanilla paste, & fold through, testing for sweetness & adding a little more icing/confectioners' sugar if you prefer.

Spoon the cheese mixture right into the piping bag & pipe blobs on top of each trifle, making sure that the jelly/jello is covered completely. Decorate with sugar dashs to serve.

ALASKA CHEESECAKES

For the crumb bases

120 g/4 ounces chocolate digestives/graham crackers

50 g/3½ tbsp butter

For the filling

2 sheets leaf gelatine

250 g/generous 1 c. Mascarpone cheese

50 g/¼ c. Caster/white sugar

80 ml/⅓ c. Passion fruit pulp, strained

125 ml/½ c. Double/heavy cream

A few drops of orange food colouring

For the sorbet

150 g/¾ c. Granulated sugar

150 g/5½ ounces dark chocolate

60 g/⅔ c. Cocoa powder, sifted

1 tsp vanilla extract

½ tsp salt

For the meringue

200 g/1 c. Caster/superfine sugar

80 ml/⅓ c. Light corn syrup

4 egg whites

8 x 6-cm/2½-inch chef's rings

An ice cream machine

A sugar thermometer

A chef's blow torch

Makes 8

For the crumb bases, crush the biscuits/graham crackers to fine crumbs in a food processor or put in a clean plastic bag & bash with a rolling pin. Transfer the crumbs to a mixing bowl & mix in the melted butter. Put the chef's rings on a baking sheet & divide the buttery crumbs between them, pressing them down firmly with the back of a spoon.

To make the filling, soak the gelatine leaves in water till they are soft.

In a big mixing bowl, whisk together the mascarpone & sugar till light & creamy, next which whisk in the passion fruit juice.

Put the cream in a heatproof bowl set over a pan of simmering water & warm gently. Squeeze the water out of the gelatine leaves & add them to the warm cream, stirring till dissolved. Pass the cream through a sieve/strainer to take away any undissolved gelatine pieces, next which whisk right into the cheese mixture with a few drops of orange food colouring, if using. Pour the cheesecake mixture right into the 8 chef's rings & leave to set in the fridge for 3 hours or overnight.

To prepare the sorbet, simmer the sugar with 500 ml/2 c. Water in a saucepan till you have a thin syrup. Add the chocolate, cocoa, vanilla & salt to the pan & simmer till the chocolate has melted. Leave to cool completely, next which churn in an ice cream machine till frozen. If you do not have an ice cream machine, transfer to a box, put in the freezer & whisk every 20 min. To break up the ice crystals till frozen. Scoop 8 round balls of sorbet & store on a tray in the freezer till you are ready to serve.

For the meringue, simmer the sugar & syrup together with 110 ml/⅓ c. Water till the sugar has dissolved, next which bring to the boil and, utilizing a sugar thermometer, heat the syrup to 115°c or soft ball stage.

In a clean dry bowl, whisk the egg whites to stiff peaks, next which add the hot sugar syrup in a small drizzle whisking continuously. Whisk for about 10–15 min. Till the meringue starts to cool.

When you are ready to serve, take away the cheesecakes from the rings by sliding a sharp knife around the edge of each. Put each on a heatproof serving plate & top with a scoop of sorbet. Working quickly, spread the meringue around each cheesecake utilizing a pallet knife, next which caramelize it with the chef's blow torch or brown under a grill/broiler. Serve straight away!

MINI POPCORN CHEESECAKES

For the crumb bases

80 g/3 ounces digestive biscuits/graham crackers

50 g/2 ounces toffee-covered popcorn

70 g/5 tbsp butter, melted

For the filling

250 g/generous 1 c. Cream cheese

250 g/generous 1 c. Mascarpone cheese

2 small eggs

1 tsp vanilla bean paste or vanilla extract

200 g/scant 1 c. Condensed milk

For the topping

25 g/2 tbsp caster/white sugar

25 g/2 tbsp muscovado sugar

25 g/1¾ tbsp butter

80 ml/⅓ c. Double/heavy cream

50 g/2 ounces toffee-covered popcorn

A 12-hole loose-based mini cheesecake pan/muffin tin , greased

12 muffin wrappers

Makes 12

Heat up the oven to 170°c gas 3.

For the bases, crush the biscuits/graham crackers & popcorn to fine crumbs in a food processor or put in a clean plastic bag & bash with a rolling pin. Transfer the crumbs to a mixing bowl & mix in the melted butter. Put a spoonful of the crumbs in each hole of the cheesecake pan & press down firmly utilizing the end of a rolling pin or the back of a small spoon. Retain a little of the crumb mixture to dash over the cheesecakes.

For the filling, whisk together the cream cheese & mascarpone in a big mixing bowl. Add the eggs, vanilla & condensed milk & whisk again till smooth. Pour the mixture right into the 12 holes of the pan so that they are just about full. Dash the reserved crumbs over the top of each cheesecake & bake in the preheated oven for 20–25 min. Till set with a slight wobble. When cool, take away from the pan & cool down in the fridge for several hours.

For the topping, heat the sugars & butter in a saucepan till the sugars have dissolved. Add the cream & heat lightlyuntil you have a thick caramel sauce. Put to the side to cool.

When you are ready to serve, put the cheesecakes in the muffin wrappers, if using, or on a serving plate. Spoon a little of the caramel sauce over each cheesecake & top with popcorn. Serve any remaining sauce alongside for extra drizzling

BERRY SUNDAE CHEESECAKES

For the fruity layer

2 tbsp vanilla vodka

12 strawberries, quartered

For the crumbly layer

8 oreo cookies

1 generous tbsp butter, melted

For the cheesecake layer

125 g/½ c. Mascarpone cheese

125 ml/½ c. Crème fraîche

1 tsp vanilla bean paste

1 generous tbsp icing/confectioners' sugar

To assemble

150 ml/⅔ c. Double/heavy cream, whipped

Chocolate dashs

6 small glasses

A piping bag fitted with a round nozzle/tip

A piping bag fitted with a star nozzle/tip

Makes 6

If utilizing the vodka, put the chopped strawberries in a bowl, pour over the vodka & leave to macerate, covered with cling film/plastic wrap, for about 20 min..

To make the crumbly layer, crush the oreo cookies to fine crumbs in a food processor or put in a clean plastic bag & bash with a rolling pin. Transfer the crumbs to a mixing bowl & mix in the melted butter, ensuring that all the crumbs are covered.

In a big mixing bowl, whisk together the mascarpone cheese & crème fraîche, next which beat in the vanilla bean paste & icing/confectioners' sugar. Spoon the cheese mixture right into the piping bag fitted with the round nozzle/tip, if using.

Place a tsp of the cookie crumb mixture in the base of each glass. Pipe in a small amount of the cream cheese mixture & top with a tsp of strawberry pieces. Continue to layer up the cheesecakes till you have filled the glasses, next which cool down in the fridge till you are ready to serve.

To serve, spoon the whipped cream right into the piping bag fitted with the star nozzle/tip & pipe a swirl of cream on top of each sundae, next which decorate with chocolate dashs. When chilled, they are best eaten the day they are made.

VALENTINE HEART CHEESECAKES

For the meringue hearts

3 egg whites

170 g/scant 1 c. Caster/superfine sugar

A few drops of pink food colouring gel

For the filling

250 g/generous 1 c. Mascarpone cheese

200 ml/generous ¾ c. Crème fraîche

100 g/⅓ c. Cherry compôte

2 tbsp icing/confectioners' sugar, sifted

To assemble

6 tbsp cherry compôte

Crystallized rose petals, shredded

A 6-hole silicone heart mould

A big baking sheet lined with baking parchment or a silicone mat

A piping bag fitted with a big round nozzle/tip

Makes 6

Heat up the oven to 140°c gas 1.

Put the egg whites in a big mixing bowl & whisk till they hold stiff peaks. Add the sugar, a tbspful at a time, whisking continously, till the meringue is shiny & glossy. Fold through the food colouring, stopping before it is fully incorporated to leave pretty swirls in the meringue.

Spoon the meringue right into the piping bag & pipe 12 heart shapes, about 7 cm/3 in. In length onto the baking sheets. Bake the hearts in the preheated oven for about 1–1¼ hours till the meringue is dried & crisp, next which leave to cool.

For the cheesecake filling, whisk together the mascarpone & crème fraîche in a big mixing bowl. Fold the cherry compôte right into the cheese mixture along with the icing/confectioners' sugar. Spoon the mixture right into each heart in the mould & put in the freezer.

When frozen, pop the hearts out of the mould & leave to defrost slightly. Put a spoonful of cherry compôte onto 6 of the meringues & top each with a cheesecake heart. Put a sec. Meringue heart on top of the cheesecake & decorate with shredded rose petals to serve.

JELLY & CUSTARD CHEESECAKE

For the topping

135 g-packet strawberry jelly cubes/3-ounces box strawberry jello powder

1 tsp vanilla bean paste

150 ml/⅔ c. Double/heavy cream, whipped to stiff peaks

8 strawberries, hulled & sliced, plus 1 whole strawberry

Sugar dashs, to decorate

For the crumb base

200 g/7 ounces pink wafer biscuits

60 g/4 tbsp butter, melted

For the cheesecake

4 sheets leaf gelatine

300 g/1⅓ c. Cream cheese

250 g/generous 1 c. Mascarpone cheese

100 g/½ c. Vanilla sugar

180 ml/¾ c. Double/heavy cream

1 generous tbsp custard powder/vanilla pudding mix

An 18-cm/7-inch ring silicone jelly mould

A 23-cm/9-inch round springform cake pan, greased & lined

A piping bag fitted with a star nozzle/tip

Serves 10

Start by preparing the jelly/jello topping. You need to do this the day before you want to serve the cheesecake as it is best to set overnight. Make up the jelly/jello according to the package instructions & mix the vanilla right into the liquid. Pour the jelly/jello right into the mould & leave to set.

For the base, crush the wafers to fine crumbs in a food processor or put in a clean plastic bag & bash with a rolling pin. Transfer the crumbs to a mixing bowl & mix in the melted butter.

Press the buttery crumbs right into the base of the prepared cake pan firmly utilizing the back of a spoon till tightly compacted.

For the filling, soak the gelatine leaves in water till they are soft.

In a big mixing bowl, whisk together the cream cheese, mascarpone & sugar till light & creamy.

Put the cream in a heatproof bowl set over a pan of simmering water & warm gently. Mix in the custard powder/vanilla pudding mix & whisk till blended. Squeeze the water from the gelatine leaves & mix them right into the cream till the gelatine dissolves. Prudently add the cream to the cream cheese mixture passing it through a sieve/strainer to take away any gelatine pieces that have not dissolved, next which beat till the mixture is smooth & slightly thick. Pour the mixture over the crumb base & cool down in the fridge for 3–4 hours or overnight till set.

When you are ready to serve, take away the cheesecake from the pan by sliding a knife around the edge of the pan & transfer the cheesecake to a serving plate. Dip the jelly/jello mould in a bowl of hot water for a few sec. To loosen the jelly/jello from the sides of the mould. Invert the jelly/jello mould on to the top of the cheesecake & take away the mould.

Spoon the whipped cream right into the piping bag & pipe stars around the edge of the cheesecake, next which pipe a little right into the middle of the jelly/jello. Arrange slices of strawberry around the edge of the jelly/jello & put the whole strawberry in the middle. Decorate with sugar dashs & serve straight away.

MACARON CHEESECAKES

For the macarons

120 g/1¼ c. Ground almonds

175 g/1¼ c. Icing/confectioners' sugar

90 g/3 ounces egg whites

75 g/generous ⅓ c. Caster/superfine sugar

Orange food colouring gel

For the crumb bases

150 g/5½ ounces digestive biscuits/graham crackers

70 g/⅔ stick butter

For the filling

2 sheets leaf gelatine

250 g/generous 1 c. Mascarpone cheese

50 g/¼ c. Caster/white sugar

Freshly squeezed juice & grated zest of 1 big orange

Freshly squeezed juice of 1 lemon

125 ml/½ c. Double/heavy cream

A few drops of orange food colouring

To assemble

1 tbsp lemon curd

200 ml/¾ c. Double/heavy cream, whipped to stiff peaks

Edible gold dusting powder

A piping bag fitted with a round nozzle/tip

2 baking sheets lined with silicone mats

A 12-hole loose-based mini cheesecake pan , greased

A piping bag fitted with a star nozzle/tip

Makes 12

For the macarons, put the ground almonds & icing/confectioners' sugar in a food processor & blitz to a very fine powder. Sift right into a bowl & return any pieces that do not pass through the sieve/strainer to the blender, blitz, next which sift again.

Whisk the egg whites to stiff peaks, next which add the caster/superfine sugar a spoonful at a time till the meringue is smooth & glossy. Add the almond mixture, a third at a time, folding in with a spatula, next which fold in the food colouring. The right texture is important – drop a little onto a plate & if it folds to a smooth surface it is ready; if it holds a peak you need to fold it a few further times. If you fold it too much it will be too runny & the macarons will not hold their shape. Spoon the mixture right into the piping bag with the round nozzle/tip & pipe 24 5-cm/2-inch rounds onto the baking sheets, with a little space around each. Leave on the sheets for 20 min. So that a skin forms on the macarons, which will give them their classic sugar-crusted edge. Heat up the oven to 170°c gas 3 & bake them for 15–20 min. Till firm. Leave to cool on the baking sheets.

To make the crumb bases, crush the biscuits/graham crackers to fine crumbs in a food processor or put in a clean plastic bag & bash with a rolling pin. Transfer the crumbs to a mixing bowl & mix in the melted butter. Divide the buttery crumbs between the holes of the cheesecake pan & press firmly down with the end of a rolling pin or the back of a spoon.

For the filling, soak the gelatine leaves in water till they are soft.

In a big mixing bowl, whisk the mascarpone & sugar together till light & creamy. Whisk in the orange & lemon juice & orange zest.

Heat the cream in a heatproof bowl set over a pan of simmering water. Squeeze the water out of the gelatine leaves & add them to the warm cream, stirring till dissolved. Pass through a sieve/strainer to take away any undissolved gelatine pieces, next which whisk right into the cheese mixture with a few drops of orange food colouring, if using. Pour the cheesecake mixture right into the holes of the pan & leave to set in the fridge for at least 3 hours.

To assemble, prudently take away the cheesecakes from the pan. Fold the lemon curd through the whipped cream & spoon right into the piping bag. Pipe a star of cream onto the base of 12 of the macarons & sandwich them with the other 12. Pipe a small dot of cream right into the middle of each cheesecake & put a filled macaron onto each. Brush the tops of the macarons with the gold dusting powder utilizing a dry pastry brush. Serve straight away or store in the fridge till needed.

TOASTED MARSHMPERMITCHEESECAKE PIE

For the crumb case

140 g/5 ounces oreo cookies

140 g/5 ounces chocolate digestive biscuits/graham crackers

6 chocolate marshmpermitteacakes

100 g/7 tbsp butter, melted

For the filling

6 sheets leaf gelatine

300 g/1⅓ c. Cream cheese

250 g/geneous 1 c. Mascarpone cheese

50 g/¼ c. Caster/white sugar

1 tsp vanilla bean paste or vanilla extract

300 ml/1¼ c. Double/heavy cream

200 g/7 ounces dark chocolate, broken right into small pieces

250 g/6–7 c. Marshmallows

A 23-cm/9-inch round springform cake pan, greased & lined

Serves 12

For the crumb case, crush all the biscuits/cookies & teacakes to fine crumbs in a food processor. Transfer the crumbs to a mixing bowl & mix in the melted butter. Press the buttery crumbs right into the base & sides of the prepared cake pan firmly utilizing the back of a spoon. You need the crumbs to come up about 3–4 cm/1½ in. High on the side of the pan so that they make a case for the filling. Make indents in the top edge of the case with your fingers to create a pretty scalloped edge.

For the filling, soak the gelatine leaves in water till they are soft.

In a big mixing bowl, whisk together the cream cheese, mascarpone, sugar & vanilla till light & creamy.

Put the cream in a heatproof bowl set over a saucepan of simmering water & heat gently. Squeeze the water from the gelatine leaves & mix them right into the warm cream till the gelatine has dissolved. Add the broken chocolate pieces to the cream & simmer till the chocolate has melted. Pass the chocolatey cream through a sieve/strainer to take away any undissolved gelatine pieces, next which whisk right into the cheese mixture till smooth. Spoon the mixture right into the crumb case & cool down in the fridge for about 3 hours or overnight till set.

When you are ready to serve, heat up the grill/broiler. Cut the marshmallows in half & arrange them over the top of the cheesecake so that they are touching. Put the cheesecake under the preheated grill/broiler for a few min. Till the marshmallows only start to caramelize. Slide a knife around the edge of the cheesecake & take away from the pan. Serve straight away.

CHEESECAKE POPS

For the cheesecake

300 g/1⅓ c. Cream cheese

150 ml/⅔ c. Sour cream

100 g/½ c. Caster/white sugar

2 eggs

1 tsp vanilla bean paste or vanilla extract

2 tsp ground cinnamon

50 g/generous ⅓ c. Self-raising flour

For the decoration

200 g/7 ounces white chocolate

200 g/7 ounces dark chocolate

Sugar dashs

A 20-cm/8-inch square loose-based cake pan, greased & lined

3 or 4-cm/1½-inch round cookie cutter

White lollipop/popsicle sticks

A silicone mat

Makes about 20

Heat up the oven to 170°c gas 3.

    To prepare the cheesecake, whisk together the cream cheese, sour cream, sugar, eggs, vanilla, cinnamon & flour in a big mixing bowl till you have a smooth creamy mixture. Pour the mixture right into the prepared cake pan & bake in the preheated oven for 35–45 min. Till the top is golden brown but still wobbles slightly in the middle. Take away from the oven & leave to cool.

    When cold, take away the cheesecake from the pan & stamp out rounds utilizing the cutter . Insert a lollipop/popsicle stick right into each cheesecake round & put them on a baking sheet. Freeze for 30 min. Or till solid.

    Melt the white chocolate in a heatproof bowl set over a pan of simmering water. Take away half the cheesecakes from the freezer & dip right into the warm chocolate. Cover with sugar dashs & leave to set on a silicone mat, if using, or sheet of non-stick baking paper. Repeat with the dark chocolate, dipping & decorating the remaining cheesecakes.

Store in the fridge till you are ready to serve.

Pear & praline push pop cheesecakes

Push pops are a new & quirky concept which are sure to bring a smile! There are quite a few steps to this recipe but they can be prepared ahead & only assembled at the last min..

For the chocolate shortcakes

100 g/¾ c. Plain/all-purpose flour

30 g/⅓ c. Cocoa powder

30 g/2½ tbsp caster/white sugar

½ tsp salt

75 g/5 tbsp butter, softened

For the pears

3 ripe pears, peeled, cored & chopped right into small pieces

Freshly squeezed juice of 1 lemon

50 g/¼ c. Sugar

For the praline & candied nuts

150 g/1 c. Macadamia nuts

150 g/¾ c. Caster/white sugar

For the filling

250 g/generous 1 c. Mascarpone cheese

250 ml/1 c. Crème fraîche

1 tsp vanilla bean paste

2 tbsp icing/confectioners' sugar, sifted

A cookie cutter slightly smaller than the diameter of the push pops

12 wooden skewers

A silicone mat

A piping bag fitted with a star nozzle/tip

12 push pops

Makes 12

For the shortcakes, sift the flour & cocoa powder in a big mixing bowl & mix in the sugar & salt. Rub the butter right into the mixture with your finger tips till you have a soft dough, adding a little more flour if the mixture is too sticky. Wrap the dough in cling film/plastic wrap & cool down in the fridge for 30 min.. In the meantime, heat up the oven to 180°c gas 4.

Roll out the dough thinly on a sheet of non-stick baking paper & transfer the paper to a baking sheet. Bake for 10–12 min. Till firm but still slightly soft. Let the shortcake cool for a few min., next which stamp out 24 rounds with the cutter. Leave the cookies to cool.

Simmer the pear pieces in a saucepan with the lemon juice, sugar & 60 ml/¼ c. Water till the pears are soft but still hold their shape . Strain off the liquid & leave the pears to cool.

For the praline, insert 12 of the macadamia nuts onto the skewers & put to the side. Put the remaining nuts closely together on a silicone mat or greased baking sheet. Heat the sugar in a heavy-based saucepan till it caramelizes . Do not mix the sugar but lightlyshake the pan to prevent it from burning. Pour two thirds of the sugar over the nuts & leave to set. Permitthe remaining sugar to cool slightly till it becomes tacky & threads pull when you lift up a spoon from it. One at a time, dip the skewered nuts right into the sugar, covering completely & next which pull upwards so that a thread of caramel pulls from the top of the nut. Let the caramel set for a few min. With the nut held downwards . If the caramel in the pan becomes too solid, simply return to the heat for a few sec., next which continue as before. When cool, take away the whole macadamias from the sticks & store in an airtight container till you are ready to assemble. Blitz the sheet of praline nuts in a food processor to make fine praline crumbs.

For the cheesecake filling, whisk together the mascarpone, crème fraiche, vanilla & icing/confectioners' sugar till the mixture thickens & holds a soft peak when you lift up the beater. Spoon the mixture right into the piping bag.

When you are ready to serve, assemble the push pops. Ensure that the push up part is correctly inserted right into the base of each pop container. Spoon a few pieces of pear right into the base of each push pop, dash with praline dust, pipe in some of the cheesecake filling, next which cover with a shortcake. Repeat the layers, ending with a cream star on top of each pop. Put one of the caramelized macadamias on top of each pop – insert the push stick & serve straight away.

AMERICAN PUMPKIN CHEESECAKE

For the base

200 g/7 ounces digestive biscuits/graham crackers

100 g/7 tbsp butter, melted

For the filling

600 g/2⅔ c. Cream cheese

225 g/1 c. Clotted cream

160 ml/⅔ c. Double/heavy cream

100 g/½ c. Caster/white sugar

425 g/1¾ c. Pumpkin purée

4 eggs

2 tsp ground cinnamon

1 tsp mixed/apple pie spice

1 tsp vanilla bean paste

To serve

Icing/confectioners' sugar & ground cinnamon, for dusting

Whipped cream

A 26-cm/10-inch round springform cake pan, greased & lined

Serves 12

Heat up the oven to 170°c gas 3.

To make the crumb base, crush the biscuits/graham crackers to fine crumbs in a food processor or put in a clean plastic bag & bash with a rolling pin. Transfer the crumbs to a mixing bowl & mix in the melted butter. Press the buttery crumbs right into the base of the prepared cake pan firmly utilizing the back of a spoon. Wrap the outside of the pan in cling film/plastic wrap & put in a roasting pan half full with water, ensuring that the water is not so high as to spill out. Put to the side.

For the filling, whisk together the cream cheese, clotted cream, double/heavy cream, sugar, pumpkin purée, eggs, cinnamon, mixed/apple pie spice & vanilla bean paste in a blender or with an electric whisk. Pour the mixture over the crumb base & transfer the cheesecake, in its waterbath, to the preheated oven. Bake in the preheated oven for 45–60 min. Till the cheesecake is set but still wobbles slightly in the middle. Turn the oven off & leave the cheesecake in the oven till cool. Cool down in the fridge for at least 3 hours, next which dust the top with icing/confectioners' sugar & cinnamon to serve.

Tip: to prepare your own pumpkin purée, peel & chop pumpkin or butternut squash, next which wrap in foil with a little water & a drizzle of maple syrup. Roast in a moderate oven till the flesh is soft, next which purée in a food processor till smooth.

FLORENTINE CHEESECAKES

For the florentines

15 glacé/candied cherries

80 g/1 c. Flaked/slivered almonds

100 g/¾ c. Golden or flame raisins

30 g/¼ c. Plain/all-purpose flour

80 ml/⅓ c. Condensed milk

2 tbsp melted butter

1 tsp ground cinnamon

1 tsp vanilla bean paste

For the filling

250 g/generous 1 c. Cream cheese

250 g/generous 1 c. Ricotta

200 g/scant 1 c. Condensed milk

2 eggs

80 g/3 ounces dark chocolate, melted, to serve

2 big baking sheets, greased & lined a 12-hole mini cheesecake or muffin pan, greased

Makes 12

Heat up the oven to 170°c gas 3.

Start by preparing the florentines. Chop the cherries right into quarters, next which put them in a bowl with the almonds & raisins. Sift in the flour & mix in the condensed milk, butter, cinnamon & vanilla. Put 24 small flat rounds of the mixture onto the prepared baking sheets & bake in the preheated oven for 8–12 min. Till lightly golden brown. Leave the florentines on the baking sheets to cool & leave the oven on to bake the cheesecakes, if you are preparing them straight away.

For the filling, whisk together the cream cheese, ricotta & condensed milk in a big mixing bowl, next which whisk in the eggs one at a time.

Reserve the 12 neatest florentines for the tops of the cheesecakes. Put one of the remaining florentines in the base of each hole of the cheesecake pan. If the florentines are too large, break them right into smaller pieces & press a few right into each hole. Spoon the filling mixture right into the 12 holes of the pan till they are just about full. Bake the cheesecakes in the preheated oven for 20–25 min. Till they are golden brown & still wobble slightly in the middle. Take away from the oven & leave to cool.

When cool, take away the cheesecakes from the pan, releasing the sides of the cheesecake utilizing a round-bladed knife. Spread a little melted chocolate over the top of each cheesecake & top with a florentine. Drizzle any remaining chocolate over the tops in thin lines, next which cool down in the fridge till you are ready to serve.

PINE NUT CHEESECAKE

For the crumb base

200 g/7 ounces digestive biscuits/graham crackers

100 g/7 tbsp butter, melted

100 g/¾ c. Pine nuts

For the filling

600 g/2⅔ c. Cream cheese

600 ml/2½ c. Crème fraîche

Freshly squeezed juice & grated zest of 2 lemons & 1 lime

60 ml/¼ c. Runny honey

50 g/¼ c. Caster/white sugar

4 eggs

2 tbsp plain/all-purpose flour

For the topping

60 g/½ c. Pine nuts

3 tbsp honey

A 23-cm/9-inch round springform cake pan, greased & lined

Serves 12

Heat up the oven to 170°c gas 3.

To make the crumb base, crush the biscuits/graham crackers to fine crumbs in a food processor or put in a clean plastic bag & bash with a rolling pin. Transfer the crumbs to a mixing bowl & mix in the melted butter & pine nuts. Press the buttery crumbs right into the base of the prepared cake pan firmly utilizing the back of a spoon. Wrap the outside of the pan in cling film/plastic wrap & put in a roasting pan half full with water, ensuring that the water is not so high as to spill out. Put to the side.

For the filling, whisk together the cream cheese, crème fraîche & the juice & zest of the lemons & lime in a big mixing bowl. Beat in the honey, sugar & eggs, next which mix in the flour.

Pour the mixture over the crumb base & transfer the cheesecake, in its waterbath, to the preheated oven. Bake for 1–1¼ hours till golden brown on top & still with a slight wobble in the middle. Take away the cheesecake from the waterbath & slide a knife around the edge of the pan to release the cheesecake & prevent it from cracking. Leave to cool, next which transfer to the fridge to cool down for at least 3 hours or preferably overnight.

For the topping, toast the pine nuts in a dry frying pan till lightly golden brown & dash over the cheesecake. Heat the honey till only warm, next which spoon over the cheesecake & serve.

CRÈME BRÛLÉE CHEESECAKES

For the crumb bases

120 g/4 ounces caramelized biscuits/cookies

60 g/4 tbsp butter, melted

For the filling

2 sheets leaf gelatine

250 g/generous 1 c. Mascarpone cheese

60 g/scant ⅓ c. Caster/white sugar

125 ml/½ c. Double/heavy cream

1 tsp vanilla bean paste

Caster/superfine sugar, to decorate

8 x 6-cm/2½-inch diameter chef's rings a chef's blow torch

Makes 8

For the bases, crush the biscuits/cookies to fine crumbs in a food processor or put in a clean plastic bag & bash with a rolling pin. Transfer the crumbs to a mixing bowl & mix in the melted butter. Placethe chef's rings on a baking sheet & divide the crumbs evenly between the rings, pressing them down flat with the back of a spoon.

For the filling, soak the gelatine leaves in water till they are soft.

In a big mixing bowl, whisk together the mascarpone & sugar till light & creamy.

Heat the cream & vanilla in a heatproof bowl set over a pan of simmering water. Squeeze the water out of the gelatine leaves & add them to the warm cream, stirring till dissolved. Pass the cream through a sieve/strainer to take away any undissolved gelatine pieces, next which whisk right into the cheese mixture. Pour the filling mixture right into the 8 rings & leave to set in the fridge for 3 hours or overnight.

When you are ready to serve, take away the cheesecakes from the rings by sliding a knife around the edge of each ring to release them. Put the cheesecakes in the freezer for 20 min. To firm. Take away from the freezer & dash the top of each cheesecake with a thin layer of sugar. Heat the sugar with the blow torch till it caramelizes, taking care not to overheat the cheesecakes otherwise they will start to melt. Let the cheesecakes come to room temperature before serving.

ROSE & CARDAMOM CHEESECAKE

For the cake base

115 g/¾ c. Shelled pistachios

60 g/scant ⅓ c. Caster/white sugar

60 g/4 tbsp butter, softened

2 eggs

60 g/scant ½ c. Self-raising flour

For the filling

6 sheets leaf gelatine

500 g/generous 2 c. Ricotta

250 g/generous 1 c. Mascarpone cheese

100 g/½ c. Caster/white sugar

25 cardamom pods

300 g/1⅓ c. Evaporated milk

160 ml/⅔ c. Double/heavy cream

80 ml/⅓ c. Rosewater

A few drops of pink food colouring

For the decoration

Crystallized rose petals

2 tbsp bright green pistachios, chopped

Edible glitter

A 23-cm/9-inch round springform cake pan, greased & lined

Serves 12

Heat up the oven to 180°c gas 4.

For the base, finely chop the pistachios in a food processor or blender.

In a big mixing bowl, whisk together the sugar & butter till creamy. Add the egg & beat again. Sift in the flour, add the ground pistachios & whisk well so that everything is incorporated. Pour the mixture right into the prepared baking pan & bake in the preheated oven for 15–20 min.

Till the cake is golden brown & springs back when pressed lightly in the middle. Leave to cool in the pan.

For the cheesecake, soak the gelatine leaves in water till they are soft.

Whisk the ricotta, mascarpone cheese & sugar together till light & creamy. Crush the cardamom pods to take away the husks, next which grind the black seeds to a fine powder in a pestle & mortar.

Heat the evaporated milk & cream together in a saucepan with the ground cardamom & rosewater & continue heating till the mixture has reduced by one third. Take away from the heat & leave to cool slightly. Squeeze the water out of the gelatine leaves & add them to the warm cream, stirring till dissolved. Pass the cream through a sieve/strainer to take away any undissolved gelatine pieces, next which whisk right into the cheese mixture with a few drops of pink food colouring, if using. Pour the filling on top of the pistachio cake base in the pan & leave to set in the fridge for 3 hours or overnight.

When you are ready to serve, arrange the crystallized rose petals on top of the cheesecake & dash with chopped pistachios & edible glitter, if using.

CRYSTALLIZED FLOWER CHEESECAKES

For the crystallized flowers

1 egg white

Pesticide-free edible flowers, stems removed

Caster/superfine sugar for sprinkling

For the crumb bases

80 g/3 ounces digestive biscuits/graham crackers

40 g/3 tbsp butter, melted

For the filling

2 sheets leaf gelatine

250 g/generous 1 c. Mascarpone cheese

60 g/scant ⅓ c. Caster/white sugar

125ml/½ c. Double/heavy cream

2 tsp culinary lavender

A small paint brush

6 glass serving dishes

A silicone mat

Makes 6

Start by preparing the sugar flowers. Whisk the egg white till it is foamy. Working on one flower at a time, use the brush to paint the egg white on both the front & the back of the flower. Dash it with caster/superfine sugar. It is important that all the egg white is covered in sugar. Repeat with all the flowers & lay on a silicone mat or sheet of non-stick baking paper placed in a warm put to dry overnight. When dried, stored the flowers in an airtight container till you are ready to serve.

To make the crumb bases, crush the biscuits/graham crackers to fine crumbs in a food processor or put in a clean plastic bag & bash with a rolling pin. Transfer the crumbs to a mixing bowl & mix in the melted butter. Press the buttery crumbs firmly right into the base of each dish utilizing the back of a spoon.

For the filling, soak the gelatine leaves in water till they are soft.

In a big mixing bowl, whisk the mascarpone & sugar together till light & creamy.

Put the cream in a heatproof bowl set over a pan of simmering water. Add the lavender & heat lightlyfor about 5 min. Till the cream has taken the lavender flavour, next which pass the cream through a sieve/strainer to take away the lavender buds. Reheat the cream till it is only warm. Squeeze the water out of the gelatine leaves & add them to the warm cream, stirring till the gelatine has dissolved. Pass the cream through a sieve/strainer a sec. Time to take away any undissolved gelatine pieces, next which whisk it right into the cheese mixture. Pour the cheesecake mixture right into the glasses & cool down in the fridge for at least 3 hours.

When you are ready to serve, decorate each cheesecake with the crystallized flowers.

PROFITEROLE CHEESECAKE

For the base

250 g/9 ounces digestive biscuits/graham crackers

100 g/7 tbsp butter, melted

For the filling

300 g/1⅓ c. Cream cheese

400 ml/1¾ c. Crème fraîche

80 g/scant ½ c. Caster/white sugar

2 eggs

1 tsp vanilla bean paste

For the profiteroles

65 g/½ c. Plain/all-purpose flour

50 g/3½ tbsp butter

2 eggs, beaten

For the patisserie cream

1 tbsp cornflour/cornstarch

60 g/⅓ c. Caster/white sugar

1 egg, plus 1 egg yolk

100 ml/generous ⅓ c. Milk

150 ml/⅔ c. Double/heavy cream

1 tsp vanilla extract

To assemble

200 ml/¾ c. Double/heavy cream

80 g/scant ½ c. Caster/white sugar

A 23-cm/9-inch round springform cake pan, greased & lined

A baking sheet, greased & lined

A piping bag fitted with a big round nozzle/tip

Serves 14

Heat up the oven to 170°c gas 3.

For the base, crush the biscuits/graham crackers to fine crumbs in a food processor or put in a clean plastic bag & bash with a rolling pin. Transfer the crumbs to a mixing bowl & mix in the melted butter. Press the crumbs right into the base of the cake pan firmly utilizing the back of a spoon.

For the filling, whisk together the cream cheese, crème fraîche & sugar. Whisk in the eggs & vanilla, next which pour over the crumb base. Bake in the preheated oven for 40–50 min. Till golden brown on top but still has a slight wobble in the middle. Leave to cool, next which transfer to the fridge to cool down for at least 3 hours or preferably overnight.

For the profiteroles, heat up the oven to 200°c gas 6. Sift the flour twice to take away any lumps. Heat the butter and 150 ml/⅔ c. Water in a saucepan till the butter is melted. Bring to the boil, next which add the flour, take away from the heat & beat hard with a wooden spoon till the dough forms a ball & no longer sticks to the pan sides. Leave to cool for about 5 min.. Whisk the eggs right into the pastry, a little at a time, to form a sticky paste. Spoon right into the piping bag & pipe 45 small balls onto the baking sheet. Wet your finger & smooth down any peaks next which bake in the oven for 12 min.. Take away from the oven & cut a small slit right into each bun & return to the oven for 3–5 min. Till crisp. Leave to cool on a rack.

For the pâtisserie cream, whisk together the cornflour/cornstarch, sugar, egg & egg yolk till creamy. Put the milk, cream & the vanilla in a saucepan & bring to the boil. Pour over the egg mixture, whisking all the time. Return to the pan & cook for a few min. Till thickened. Pass through a sieve/strainer to take away any lumps, next which leave to cool.

To assemble the cheesecake, whisk the 200 ml/⅔ c. Cream to stiff peaks, next which fold through the pâtisserie cream. Spread some of the pâtisserie cream over the top of the cheesecake & spoon the remaining right into the piping bag. Fill each profiterole with the cream, piping it right into the slit in the profiterole, next which arrange them in rings on top of the cheesecake.

For the spun sugar, heat the sugar in a heavy-based saucepan till it caramelizes . Do not mix the sugar but lightlyshake the pan to prevent it from burning. Permitthe caramel to cool slightly till the sugar becomes tacky & threads pull when you lift up a spoon from it. Pull threads of caramel by starting with some of the slightly cooled caramel on a spoon & allowing a drip to fall to create a sugar thread, next which keep pulling the thread with your fingers to create the spun sugar. If the caramel becomes too solid, simply return to the heat for a few sec. & next which continue as before. Wrap the spun sugar right into a ball & put on top of the profiteroles. Serve straight away

ALMOND CHEESECAKE

For the nutty crust

150 g/scant 2 c. Flaked/slivered almonds

30 g/2 tbsp butter, softened

For the filling

500 g/generous 2 c. Cream cheese

500 g/generous 2 c. Ricotta

4 big eggs

400 g/1¾ c. Condensed milk

80 g/⅓ c. Almond butter

1 tsp almond extract

For the topping

80 g/¾ stick butter

120 g/½ c. Golden marzipan

100 g/scant 1 c. Crushed amaretti biscuits/cookies

A 23-cm/9-inch round springform cake pan, greased & lined

Serves 12

In a dry frying pan set over a gentle heat, toast the flaked/slivered almonds till lightly golden brown, watching prudently as almonds can burn quickly. Tip right into a bowl & put to the side to cool completely.

Spread the softened butter around the sides & base of the prepared cake pan. Dash the cooled toasted almonds right into the pan & shake it so that the base & sides of the pan are covered with almonds.

Heat up the oven to 170°c gas 3.

In a big mixing bowl, whisk together the cream cheese & ricotta, next which add the eggs, condensed milk, almond butter & almond extract & whisk till the mixture is smooth. Spoon the mixture right into the almond-covered pan & bake in the preheated oven for 45 min..

Whilst the cheesecake is baking, prepare the topping. Melt the butter in a saucepan. Chop the marzipan right into small pieces & mix with the crushed amaretti biscuits/cookies. Pour over the warm melted butter & mix together. For best results do this with your hands so that the biscuits/cookies & marzipan stick together in small clumps.

After 45 min. Baking time, the cheesecake should be golden brown on top & still wobble slightly in the middle. Prudently dash the marzipan crumbs over the top of the cheesecake . Bake for a further 15 min. Till the topping is crunchy & the marzipan has caramelized. Take away the cheesecake from the oven & slide a knife lightlyaround the edge of the pan to loosen the cheesecake & prevent it from cracking. Leave to cool, next which cool down in the fridge for at least 3 hours or overnight before serving.

CHEESECAKE CHOCOLATES

For the cake bases

55 g/4 tbsp butter

55 g/4½ tbsp caster/white sugar

1 egg

55 g/scant ½ c. Self-raising flour

Grated zest of 1 orange

For the drizzling syrup

Freshly squeezed juice of 1 orange

1 tbsp icing/confectioners' sugar

For the filling

170 g/¾ c. Mascarpone cheese

170 ml/¾ c. Crème fraîche

1 tbsp icing/confectioners' sugar

1 tsp vanilla bean paste

To assemble

400 g/14 ounces dark spiced chocolate

24 sugar flowers

A 24-hole square mini brownie pan, greased

A piping bag fitted with a round nozzle/tip

24 paper petit fours cases

Makes 24

Heat up the oven to 180°c gas 4.

To make the cake bases, whisk together the butter & sugar in a big mixing bowl, till light & creamy. Beat in the egg & whisk again. Sift in the flour, add half of the orange zest & mix through again. Put a small spoonful of mixture right into each of the holes of the prepared brownie pan. You only want a little cake mixture in each hole as when the cakes are baked you still need room to add the cheesecake mixture on top. Bake in the preheated oven for 10–12 min. Till the sponges spring back when you press with a clean finger.

Simmer the orange juice & sugar in a saucepan till the sugar has dissolved, next which drizzle a little of the syrup over each of the cakes. Leave the cakes to cool, next which press the cakes down so that there is room for the filling on top.

For the cheesecake filling, whisk together the mascarpone, crème fraîche, icing/confectioners' sugar, vanilla & the remaining orange zest till smooth. Spoon the mixture over the cake bases, spreading in tightly utilizing a pallet knife or spatula so that all the holes of the brownie pan are filled completely. Transfer the pan to the freezer & freeze till the cheesecake is solid, which will take about 30 min..

When the cheesecakes are frozen, melt the dark chocolate in a heatproof bowl set over a pan of simmering water, stirring till the chocolate has melted. Take away the frozen cheesecakes from the freezer and, one at a time, dip them right into the warm chocolate. Transfer to a wire rack to set, with a sheet of foil underneath to catch any chocolate drips. Before the chocolate sets, affix a sugar flower to the top of each cheesecake. The chocolate will set quickly given the frozen temperatures of the cheesecakes – if it sets too quickly you can simply attach the flowers utilizing a little extra chocolate. When set, put each chocolate in a petit fours case & store in the fridge till you are ready to serve, by which time the cheesecake will have defrosted.

GREEK BAKLAVA CHEESECAKE

9 big sheets filo/phyllo pastry

120 g/1 stick butter, melted

3–4 tbsp runny greek honey

Pistachios, for sprinkling

For the cheesecake filling

225 g/1 c. Quark/farmer cheese

150 g/⅔ c. Cream cheese

1 small egg, plus 1 egg yolk

50 g/¼ c. Caster/white sugar

Grated zest of 1 lemon

75 g/¾ c. Ground almonds

For the nut filling

100 g/¾ c. Pistachios

50 g/¼ c. Caster/white sugar, plus extra for sprinkling

2 tsp ground cinnamon

A piping bag fitted with a big round nozzle/tip

A 23-cm/9-inch round springform cake pan or tarte tatin pan, greased & lined

Serves 10

Heat up the oven to 180°c gas 4.

To prepare the cheesecake filling, whisk together the quark/farmer cheese, cream cheese, egg & egg yolk, sugar, lemon zest & almonds in a big mixing bowl till the mixture is smooth & creamy. Spoon the mixture right into the piping bag.

For the nut filling, blitz the pistachios with the sugar & cinnamon in a food processor till finely chopped.

Take away the filo/phyllo pastry from the packet & cut the sheets in half so that you are left with 18 smaller sheets. Cover with a damp tea towel/dish towel, which will prevent it from drying out & cracking. Lay one sheet of filo/phyllo on a clean work surface & brush with the melted butter utilizing a pastry brush. Cover with a sec. Sheet of filo/phyllo & brush with butter again. Dash with a few tbsp of the nut mixture so that the whole sheet is covered in a thin layer of nuts, next which cover with a third sheet of filo/phyllo & brush again with butter. Pipe a line of the cheesecake filling along one of the long edges, next which roll up so that the filling is in the middle of each tube.

Place the filo/phyllo tube around the edge of the prepared cake pan. Repeat with the remaining pastry till you have made 6 tubes of cheesecake pastry in total. Continue to arrange them in the pan in a spiral so that the ends of each tube touch, next which brush the top of the pastry with a little more butter & bake in the preheated oven for 20–30 min. Till the top of the pastry is crisp & golden.

Heat the honey in a saucepan till it becomes thin & easily pourable next which spoon over the baklava & leave to cool completely. Dash with bright green pistachios & a little sugar, to serve.

CARDAMOM BUN CHEESECAKE

For the dough

20 cardamom pods

200 ml/¾ c. Warm milk

7 g/¼ ounces fast action yeast

30 g/2½ tbsp granulated sugar

460 g/3½ c. Plain/all-purpose flour, sifted, plus extra for dusting

½ tsp salt

2 eggs, beaten

60 g/4 tbsp butter, softened

For the filling

250 g/generous 1 c. Mascarpone cheese

1 egg

50 g/¼ c. Caster/white sugar

1 vanilla pod/bean

For the topping

250 ml/1 c. Double/heavy cream

200 g/7 ounces marzipan

Icing/confectioners' sugar, for dusting

A 34 x 24-cm/13 x 9½-inch roasting pan, greased

A piping bag fitted with a big nozzle/tip

Makes 12

For the dough, crush the cardamom pods in a pestle & mortar & take away the green husks. Grind the black seeds to a fine powder.

Place the warm milk, yeast & sugar in a jug/pitcher, whisk together & leave in a warm put for about 10 min. Till a thick foam has formed on top of the milk.

In the meantime, sift the flour right into a big mixing bowl, add the salt, eggs, butter & cardamom powder & mix together to incorporate, next which pour in the yeast mixture. Utilizing a stand mixer fitted with a dough hook, mix the dough on a slow speed for 2 min., next which increase the speed & knead for about 8 min. Till the dough is very soft & pliable. Alternatively, knead the dough by hand for about 10–15 min..

For the cheesecake filling, whisk together the mascarpone, egg & sugar in a big mixing bowl till smooth. Cut the vanilla pod/bean in half & take away the seeds utilizing the back of a knife, next which mix them right into the mixture.

With your hands, press the dough out to cover the bottom of the prepared pan, next which spread the cheesecake mixture over the top of the dough, leaving a small gap around the edge. Put the pan in a warm put for about 1 hour or till the dough has doubled in size.

Heat up the oven to 180°c gas 4.

Bake the bun in the oven for 20–30 min. Till the dough is golden brown & sounds hollow when you tap it. Leave to cool, next which slice right into 12 squares with a sharp serrated knife.

Spoon the whipped cream right into the piping bag & pipe stars of the cream on top of each cheesecake square. Utilizing a swivel vegetable peeler or sharp knife, cut thin ribbons of the marzipan & scatter on top of the cream. Dust with icing/confectioners' sugar to serve.

As this contains fresh cream, it needs to be eaten straight away or stored in the fridge. This needs to be eaten on the day it is made.

POLISH CHEESECAKE

For the pastry crust

120 g/1 stick butter, chilled

230 g/1¾ c. Plain/all-purpose flour

50 g/¼ c. Caster/white sugar

2 egg yolks

1 tbsp cream cheese

A splash of milk, to glaze

For the filling

500 g/generous 2 c. Twaróg cheese

250 g/generous 1 c. Cream cheese

4 eggs, separated

400 g/1¾ c. Condensed milk

125 g/1 stick plus 1 tbsp butter, melted

Icing/confectioners' sugar, for dusting

A deep 30 x 22-cm/12 x 9-inch roasting pan, greased

Leaf pastry cutters

Serves 14

For the pastry crust, rub the butter right into the flour till it resembles fine breadcrumbs. Add the sugar, egg yolks & cream cheese & mix together to a soft dough with your fingers, adding a little extra flour if the mixture is too sticky, or a little chilled water if it is too dry. Wrap the pastry dough in cling film/plastic wrap & cool down in the fridge for 1 hour.

Bring the dough back to room temperature and, on a lightly floured surface, roll it out to a sheet big enough to line the roasting pan. Lay the pastry right into the prepared pan & trim the edges. Roll out the trimmings & cut out small leaf shapes to decorate the cheesecake with.

Heat up the oven to 170°c gas 3.

To make the filling, pass the twaróg cheese through a fine mesh sieve/strainer. In a big mixing bowl, whisk the strained twaróg, cream cheese, eggs & condensed milk together till you have a smooth cream. Slowly pour in the melted butter, whisking all the time. Pour the mixture right into the pastry case, arrange the pastry leaves on top. Brush the leaves with a little milk, to glaze, next which bake in the preheated oven for 45–60 min. Till the cheesecake is golden brown & still wobbles slightly in the middle. Take away from the oven & leave to cool, next which cool down in the fridge before serving.

To serve, cut the chilled cheesecake right into squares & dust with icing/confectioners' sugar. This is delicious served with poached fruits.

JAPANESE CHERRY BLOSSOM CHEESECAKE

For the cake base

55 g/4 tbsp butter, softened

55 g/¼ c. Caster/white sugar

1 egg

2 tsp matcha powder

1 generous tbsp crème fraîche

55 g/scant ½ c. Self-raising flour, sifted

For the filling

4 sheets leaf gelatine

200 g/scant 1 c. Cream cheese

250 g/generous 1 c. Ricotta

1 tsp vanilla bean paste

100 g/½ c. Caster/white sugar

150 ml/⅔ c. Double/heavy cream

400 g/1½–2 c. Cherry compôte

For the decoration

30 g/1 ounces dark chocolate, melted sugar flowers

A 23-cm/9-inch round springform cake pan, greased & lined

A piping bag fitted with a small round nozzle/tip

Serves 12

Heat up the oven to 180°c gas 4.

For the cake base, whisk together the butter & sugar in a big mixing bowl till creamy. Add the egg & beat again. Dissolve the matcha powder in 1 tbsp hot water & add to the cake mixture along with the crème fraîche. Sift the flour over the mixture & fold in so that everything is incorporated. Pour the cake batter right into the prepared baking pan & bake in the preheated oven for 15–20 min. Till the cake is golden brown & springs back when pressed lightlyin the middle. Leave to cool in the pan.

For the filling, soak the gelatine leaves in water till they are soft.

In a big mixing bowl, whisk the cream cheese, ricotta, vanilla & sugar together till light & creamy.

Put the cream in a heatproof bowl set over a pan of simmering water & heat gently. Squeeze the water out of the gelatine leaves & add them to the warm cream, stirring till dissolved. Pass the cream through a sieve/strainer to take away any undissolved gelatine pieces, next which whisk right into the cheese mixture.

Blitz the cherry compôte in a blender or food processor to make a smooth purée. Spread one third of the cherry purée over the cake base, leaving a small gap around the edge of the cake. Fold the remaining cherry purée right into the cheesecake mixture, stopping before it is fully incorporated to make a pretty swirled pattern. Pour the cheesecake mixture over the base & smooth level, next which leave to set in the fridge for 3 hours or overnight.

To decorate, spoon the melted chocolate right into the piping bag & pipe delicate chocolate branches on top of the cheesecake. Fix sugar flowers to the branches utilizing a little extra chocolate so that they look like cherry blossom branches.

WHISKY & RASPBERRY CRANACHAN CHEESECAKES

For the flapjack base

50 g/3½ tbsp butter

30 g/2½ tbsp caster/white sugar

40 g/2 tbsp golden/light corn syrup

100 g/1 c. Rolled oats

A pinch of salt

For the filling

150 g/1–1¼ c. Raspberries

80 ml/⅓ c. Whisky

300 g/1⅓ c. Cream cheese

300 ml/1¼ c. Crème fraîche

80 ml/¼ c. Honey

2 eggs

Generous 1 tbsp flour, sifted

To serve

Fresh raspberries

Pouring cream

A baking sheet, greased

8 x 6-cm/2½-inch diameter chef's rings, greased & placed on a greased baking sheet

Makes 8

Heat up the oven to 170°c gas 3.

For the flapjack base, heat the butter, sugar & golden/corn syrup together in a saucepan till the butter & sugar have melted & the mixture is syrupy. Mix in the oats & salt & mix well so that all the oats are covered.

Spoon the mixture onto the prepared baking sheet & flatten with the back of a spoon. Bake in the preheated oven for 20–30 min. Till the flapjack is golden brown. Take away from the oven & leave to cool for a few min.. Whilst still warm, use one of the chef's rings to stamp out 8 rounds of flapjack to use as bases, next which leave them to cool completely. Leave the oven on.

For the filling, soak the raspberries in the whisky for 30 min..

In a big mixing bowl, whisk together the cream cheese & crème fraîche. Whisk in the honey, eggs & flour, next which fold through the raspberries & any remaining soaking whisky. Spoon the mixture right into the chef's rings on the baking sheet & bake in the preheated oven for 25–30 min. Till golden brown on top. Leave to cool next which transfer to the fridge to cool down for at least 3 hours or preferably overnight.

When you are ready to serve, put a flapjack disc on each plate & top with a cheesecake. Serve with extra fresh raspberries & cream & a tot of whisky if you wish.

BLACK FOREST CHEESECAKE

For the base

55 g/4 tbsp butter

55 g/¼ c. Caster/white sugar

1 egg

55 g/scant ½ c. Self-raising flour

15 g/2½ tsp cocoa powder

1 generous tbsp crème fraîche

2 tbsp kirsch

270 g /2 c. Morello cherries in syrup, plus 2 tbsp of the syrup

For the filling

300 g/1⅓ c. Cream cheese

250 g/generous 1 c. Ricotta

4 eggs

400 g/1¾ c. Condensed milk

200 g/7 ounces dark chocolate, melted & cooled

For the topping

250 ml/1 c. Double/heavy cream, whipped to stiff peaks

Chocolate dashs

A 20-cm/8-inch square springform cake pan, greased & lined

A piping bag fitted with a star nozzle/tip

Serves 12

Heat up the oven to 180°c gas 4.

For the base, whisk together the butter & sugar in a big mixing bowl till light & creamy. Beat in the egg & whisk again. Sift in the flour & the cocoa & fold through lightlytogether with the crème fraîche. Spoon right into the prepared cake pan & spread out evenly in a thin layer over the base. Bake in the preheated oven for 10–15 min. Till the sponge springs back when you press it with a clean finger. Permitthe sponge base to cool in the pan, next which drizzle the kirsch & cherry syrup over the base. Dash three quarters of the cherries in a layer over the base.

Heat up the oven to 160°c gas 3.

For the filling, whisk together the cream cheese & ricotta in a big mixing bowl, till smooth & creamy. Add the eggs, condensed milk & cooled melted chocolate & whisk again. Spoon the mixture right into the baking pan over the cherries & bake in the preheated oven for 1–1¼ hours till the cheesecake is set but still has a slight wobble in the middle. Leave to cool in the pan, next which refrigerate till you are ready to serve.

To serve, spread half the cream over the top of the cheesecake & decorate with the reserved cherries & chocolate dashs. Spoon the remaining cream right into the piping bag & pipe small stars of cream around the edge of the cheesecake. Serve straight away or store in the fridge till needed.

TIRAMISU CHEESECAKE

For the cake

115 g/1 stick butter

115 g/generous ½ c. Caster/white sugar

2 eggs

100 g/¾ c. Self-raising flour

15 g/2½ tsp cocoa powder

For the fill.ing

500 ml/generous 2 c. Crème fraîche

500 g/generous 2 c. Mascarpone cheese

3 tbsp icing/confectioners' sugar, or to taste

To assemble

80 ml/⅓ c. Double espresso coffee*

100 ml/⅓ c. Amaretto

50 g/2 ounces nougat chocolate , coarsely grated

Cocoa powder, for dusting

A 23-cm/9-inch round springform cake pan, greased & lined

Serves 10

*if you don't have an espresso machine, dissolve 1 tbsp coffee granules in 80 ml/⅓ c. Hot water, next which leave to cool before utilizing in the recipe.

Heat up the oven to 180°c gas 4.

For the cake, cream together the butter & sugar till light & creamy utilizing a whisk or electric mixer. Add the eggs & beat again. Sift in the flour & cocoa & fold in. Spoon the mixture right into the prepared cake pan & bake in the preheated oven for 10–15 min. Or till the cake springs back to your touch. Leave to cool completely.

For the filling, whisk together the crème fraîche & mascarpone. Sift the icing/confectioners' sugar over the mixture & fold through. Taste the mixture for sweetness & add a little further sugar if you wish.

Take away the cake from the pan & cut it in half horizontally with a sharp serrated knife. Put the bottom half of the cake back in the pan.

Mix together the coffee & amaretto. Spoon half the coffee mixture over the bottom cake, dash over half the grated chocolate & dust liberally with cocoa. Spoon half of the filling mixture right into the pan & spread out evenly utilizing a spatula, next which dust with more cocoa powder. Put the sec. Cake half on top & spoon over the remaining coffee mixture, dash with the remaining grated chocolate & dust with cocoa powder again. Spoon over the remaining filling mixture & spread level. Dust the top of the cheesecake with cocoa powder & cool down in the fridge overnight for best results.

To take away from the pan, slide a round-bladed knife around the sides of the chilled cheesecake before removing the sides of the pan, & serve.

Cheesecake tarts

Yield 14

What you need
16oz cream cheese, softened
3/4 c. Sugar
2 tbsp all-purpose flour
2 eggs
1/2 tsp vanilla extract
1/4 tsp almond extract
Vegetable cooking spray
2/3 c. Gingersnap crumbs
3 c. Assorted fresh fruit

What to do
1. Heat up oven to 350 °f .
2. Beat cream cheese till smooth. Add sugar & flour, mix well. Add eggs, one at a time whereas stirring.
3. Dash gingersnap crumbs evenly between tart pans.
4. Pour cheesecake batter evenly between tart pans.
5. Bake for 20 min.. Permit to cool & take away from tart pans.
6. Spread fruit evenly over each cheesecake tart.

Cheesecake lollipops

Yield 8

What you need
24oz cream cheese, softened
3/4 c. Sugar
1/3 c. Sour cream
3 tbsp all-purpose flour
1 tsp vanilla
1/4 tsp salt
3 eggs

24 lollipop sticks
10oz white chocolate
Chocolate chips
Toasted coconut

What to do
1. Heat up oven to 350 °f .
2. Mix cream cheese & sugar till smooth. Pour in sour cream & mix well.
3. Mix flour, vanilla & salt in the mixture. Beat eggs one at a time.
4. Pour filling right into a lightly greased 9-inch pan.
5. Bake for 50 min..
6. Turn off the oven, open the door & leave the cheesecake inside to cool. Refrigerate.
7. Take small scoops out of cheesecake. Form right into 1 1/2-inch balls & put on a lined baking sheet.
8. Attach lollipop sticks to each cheesecake ball. Put the tray in the freezer till firm.
9. Heat white chocolate till melted. Dip each cheesecake lollipop right into the chocolate.
10. Garnish lollipops with chocolate chips or toasted coconut if you wish.
11. Permit covering to set. Cool down in the fridge before serving.

Toffee cheesecake bars

What you need
16oz cream cheese
1/2 c. Brown sugar
1 tsp vanilla extract
1 tsp ground cinnamon
1/4 tsp ground nutmeg
1/4 tsp ground cloves
3/4 c. Chopped toffee bars

What to do
1. Beat cream cheese till smooth.
2. Add sugar, vanilla, cinnamon, nutmeg & cloves & blend till well incorporated.
3. Dip toffee bars in mixture & refrigerate.
4. Serve with fruits, graham crackers or pretzels.

Bittersweet apple cheesecake roll
yield 10

What you need
6 tortillas
2 tbsp butter, melted
1 tbsp granulated sugar
1 tsp cinnamon
Salted caramel sauce

Apple filling:
1 tbsp butter, melted
3 c. Apple, peeled, chopped
2 tbsp granulated sugar
1 tsp cinnamon, ground
1/4 tsp nutmeg, ground
1/4 tsp allspice, ground

Cheesecake filling:
8oz cream cheese
1/3 c. Granulated sugar
2 tbsp all-purpose flour
1/2 tsp vanilla extract

What to do
1. Heat up oven to 350 °f .
2. Melt butter over medium heat. Add chopped apples, sugar & spices. Mix well. Cook for 10 min..
3. Mix cream cheese, sugar, flour & vanilla till well incorporated.
4. Arrange tortillas at the bottom of a 9 in. Pan & spread filling over them.
5. Spread apple mixture evenly over the filling.
6. Mix together 1 tbsp granulated sugar & 1 tsp of cinnamon. Dash half of it over butter.
7. Roll tortillas & put seam down. Brush it with butter.
8. Garnish with remaining cinnamon sugar. Bake for 25 min..
9. Pour over salted caramel sauce & serve.

Cranberry cheese squares

Yield 16

What you need
Crust:
1 1/2 c. Granola
1/4 c. Butter, melted

Cheesecake:
12 ounces   cream cheese
1/2 c. Greek yoghurt
1/3 c. Sugar
2 tbsp all-purpose flour
1 tsp almond extract
2 eggs

Cranberry mixture:
3/4 c. Canned jellied cranberry sauce

Garnish:
1/3 c. Sliced almonds

What to do
1. Heat up oven to 350 °f .
2. Finely grind granola & mix with 3 tbsp sugar & the melted butter till well incorporated. Press to the bottom of an ungreased 9 in. Pan.
3. Bake for 8 min..
4. In a separate bowl, mix cream cheese, yogurt, sugar, flour, almond extract & eggs till smooth.
5. Pour cheesecake batter over the baked crust. Layer with spoonfuls of cranberry on top. Top off with almonds.
6. Bake for 40 min. & permit to cool afterwards.
7. Cool down in the fridge before cutting right into squares.

Banana cheesecake

Yield 10

What you need
20 vanilla cream-filled sandwich style cookies, finely chopped
1/4 c. Butter, melted
24oz cream cheese, softened
2/3 c. Granulated sugar
2 tbsp cornstarch
3 eggs
3/4 c. Mashed banana
1/2 c. Whipping cream
2 tsp vanilla extract
Coconut, for topping

What to do
1. Heat up oven to 350 °f .
2. Blend cookies & margarine. Mix well. Press to the bottom of a lightly greased 10 in. Pan.
3. Mix cream cheese, sugar & cornstarch. Add eggs one at a time.
4. Add bananas, whipping cream & vanilla. Pour filling right into crust.
5. Bake for 15 min.. Reduce temperature to 200 °f & bake for 75 min.. Permit to cool.
6. Refrigerate.

Chocolate truffle cheesecake

Yield 10

What you need
1 1/2 c. Chocolate- cookies, crushed
2 tbsp butter, melted
8oz semisweet chocolate bars, chopped
1 c. Whipping cream
32oz packages cream cheese, softened
14oz sweetened condensed milk

2 tsp vanilla extract
4 eggs
Fresh raspberries

What to do
1. Heat up oven to 300 °f.
2. Mix crushed cookies & butter. Press mixture to the bottom of a 9-inch springform pan.
3. Microwave chocolate & cream till melted, stirring at 30-second intervals.
4. Beat cream cheese till smooth.
5. Add sweetened condensed milk & vanilla & mix well. Add eggs one at a time. Pour in chocolate mixture. Mix well.
6. Pour mixture right into crust.
7. Bake 1 hour & 5 min.. Turn off the oven, open the door & leave the cheesecake inside to cool for 30 min.
8. Refrigerate overnight.
9. Top with fresh raspberries.

Chocomint cheesecake

Yield 10

What you need
8oz cream cheese, softened
3 tbsp granulated sugar
1/2 tsp vanilla extract
1/8 tsp peppermint extract
8oz frozen whipped topping, thawed
12 mint chocolate cookies, finely chopped

What to do
1. Mix cream cheese & sugar till smooth & creamy. Add extracts & mix well.
2. Fold whipped topping right into cream cheese mixture. Add mint chocolate cookies.
3. Pour filling right into pastry bag. Cut the end of the bag & pipe batter right into serving glasses.
4. Alternate layers of the cookies & cream cheese mixture with chopped cookies.
5. Top with additional whipped topping & chopped cookies.

Green tea mousse cheesecake

Yield 12

What you need
4.8oz graham crackers, crushed
2 tbsp white sugar
3 tbsp butter, melted
2 tbsp green tea powder
1/2 c. Warm water
2 tbsp gelatin
1/2 c. Cold water
2 c. Whipping cream
16oz cream cheese
1/2 c. White sugar
1 tsp vanilla extract
1/4 c. Honey
2 eggs

What to do
1. Mix graham cracker crumbs, 2 tbsp sugar & butter.
2. Press to the bottom of a lightly greased 9 in. Pan.
3. Mix matcha powder right into warm water. Put to the side.
4. Dash gelatin over cold water. Put to the side.
5. Beat the cream to stiff peaks; put to the side.
6. Mix together cream cheese, 1/2 c. Sugar, vanilla, & honey in a bowl.
7. Add in the eggs one at a time.
8. Cook the gelatin mixture in the microwave till melted.
9. Pour gelatin & tea right into cream cheese mixture, next which add in whipped cream till smooth.
10. Pour batter over pan.
11. Refrigerate overnight.

Frozen blueberry & lime cheesecake

Yield 12

What you need
3 limes
2oz caster sugar
8.8oz blueberries

Cheesecake:
3 egg whites
5oz confectioners' sugar
8.8oz mascarpone
1/2 tsp vanilla extract
10oz double cream

Crust:
8.8oz amaretti biscuits
2oz butter

What to do
1. Grate the lime zest. Put to the side.
2. Squeeze the juice from the limes right into a pan. Add sugar & blueberries & heat till sugar dissolves. Simmer for 1-2 min..
3. Take away blueberries & put to the side. Reduce juice till slightly thickened. Pour over the blueberries & put to the side.
4. Beat egg whites till stiff, add confectioners' sugar till it forms soft peaks.
5. Mix mascarpone, lime zest & vanilla. Whip the cream & fold right into the mascarpone. Fold in egg white mixture.
6. Crush the amaretti biscuits right into crumbs & mix with melted butter. Press to the bottom of a lightly greased pan.
7. Spread the blueberries & juice over the base. Spread the cheesecake mixture over the blueberries. Dash the amaretti crumbs over the top.
8. Freeze.

Salted caramel ginger snap cheesecake

Yield 12

What you need

Cheesecake:
3 1/2 c. Ginger snaps, finely ground
1/2 c. Almonds, ground
2/3 c. Butter, melted
1 1/2 c. Ricotta cheese
16oz cream cheese
1 c. Brown sugar
4 eggs
2 tbsp golden syrup
1/4 tsp salt
1 tsp vanilla extract

Sauce:
1 c. Whipping cream
1/4 c. Butter, cubed
1 c. Brown sugar

Topping:
1 c. Whipping cream
1 c. Sour cream
1 tsp vanilla
1 tbsp confectioners' sugar, sifted
Sea salt

What to do
Cheesecake:
1. Heat up oven to 325 °f .
2. Mix ginger snaps, almonds & butter. Mix till well incorporated. Press to the bottom of a lightly greased 8 in. Pan.
3. Refrigerate.
4. Beat ricotta & cream cheese in a bowl till smooth. Mix in sugar & mix well.
5. Add the eggs one at a time. Add syrup, salt & vanilla. Scoop mixture over the crust.
6. Bake for an hour & a half. Refrigerate.
7. Garnish cheesecake with the cream, drizzle with the caramel sauce & dash with sea salt flakes.

Sauce:
1. Mix cream, butter & sugar in a saucepan over low heat & mix till sugar is dissolved.
2. Increase & bring to boil & cook for till thickened & becomes the color of caramel. Permit to cool.

Topping:
Beat together cream, sour cream, confectioners' sugar & vanilla in a bowl.

Coffee cheesecake

Yield 12

What you need
8 whole graham crackers, crushed
5 tbsp butter, melted
1 1/2 c. Sugar
1/2 c. Whipping cream
4 tsp instant coffee powder
1 1/2 tsp vanilla extract
8oz cream cheese
2 tbsp all-purpose flour
1 c. Semi-sweet chocolate chips
Chocolate, shaved right into curls

What to do
1. Heat up oven to 350 °f .
2. Mix graham crackers, butter & 1/4 c. Sugar. Press to the bottom of a lightly greased 9 in. Pan.
3. Bake for 10 min.. Permit to cool.
4. Blend cream cheese, coffee & vanilla.
5. Beat cream cheese, 1 1/4 c. Sugar & add eggs one at a time. Mix in flour.
6. Mix espresso mixture & pour right into cream cheese mixture. Add chocolate chips.
7. Pour mixture over crust. Bake for an hour.
8. Permit to cool. Refrigerate overnight.
9. Garnish with chocolate curls.

Chocolate melt cheesecake

Yield 10

What you need
1 1/2 c. Vanilla wafer crumbs, crushed
1/2 c. Powdered sugar
1/3 c. Cocoa
1/3 c. Butter, melted
24oz cream cheese, softened
14oz sweetened condensed milk
2 c. Semi-sweet chocolate chips, melted
4 eggs
2 tsp vanilla extract
Whipped cream
More chocolate chips

What to do
1. Heat up oven to 300 °f .
2. Blend vanilla wafer crumbs, powdered sugar, cocoa & butter.
2. Press mixture to the bottom of a lightly greased 9 in. Pan. Put to the side.
3. Beat cream cheese till fluffy. Slowly add milk whereas beating.
4. Pour melted chocolate chips, egg & vanilla. Pour mixture right into crust.
5. Put cheesecake pan in a larger baking pan with warm water midway up the sides & bake for an hour.
6. Take away & permit to cool. Serve.

Mint cheesecake

Yield 12

What you need
12oz oreos, crushed
3 tbsp butter
24oz cream cheese
3/4 c. Sugar
1/3 c. Sour cream
4 eggs
2 tbsp all-purpose flour

1 tsp vanilla extract
1/2 tsp peppermint extract
1/2 tsp salt
1/3 c. Candy cane, crushed

What to do
1. Heat up oven to 300 °f .
2. Blend together oreo crumbs & butter. Press to the bottom of a lightly greased 9 in. Pan.
3. Bake crust for 10 min..
4. Beat cream cheese till smooth. Add sour cream. Add eggs in one at a time. Add flour, vanilla, peppermint extract & salt & beat till smooth.
5. Pour filling over baked crust.
6. Bake for an hour. Permit to cool afterwards & refrigerate.
7. Garnish with candy cane.

Toffee truffle cheesecake

Yield 8

What you need
Crust:
1 1/2 c. Graham cracker crumbs
1/2 c. Toasted almond, finely chopped
1/2 c. Toffee pieces
2 tbsp dark brown sugar
1/4 tsp salt
6 tbsp butter, melted

Filling:
32oz cream cheese
1 c. Packed dark brown sugar
4 eggs
1 tbsp vanilla extract
1/4 tsp almond extract
8oz chocolate-covered toffee bars, chopped

Topping:
16oz sour cream
1/2 c. Sugar
1 tsp vanilla extract
Extra crushed chocolate-covered toffee bar, for sprinkling

What to do
1. Heat up oven to 350 °f.
2. Mix graham cracker crumbs, toasted almonds, toffee pieces, dark brown sugar, salt & butter.
3. Press to the bottom of a lightly greased 10 in. Pan
4. Bake for 5 min.. Take away from oven & reduce temperature to 325 °f.
5. Mix cream cheese & sugar. Add eggs one at a time.
6. Pour half of the batter right into the baked crust. Dash with toffee pieces.
7. Pour the other half of the mixture over the toffee pieces.
8. Bake for an hour.
9. Mix topping ingredients till smooth. Pour over cheesecake.
10. Permit to cool & refrigerate. Garnish with crushed toffee.

Lime cheesecake

Yield 8

What you need
1 1/4 c. Graham cracker crumbs
1/4 c. Sugar
3 tbsp butter, melted
24oz cream cheese
1 1/4 c. Sugar
4 eggs
1 1/2 tbsp lime juice
1 pinch salt

What to do
1. Heat up oven to 350 °f.
2. Mix graham cracker crumbs, sugar & melted butter in a bowl. Press to the bottom of a lightly greased 9 in. Pan.

3. Bake for 10 min.. Take away from oven & permit to cool.
4. Mix together cream cheese, sugar & eggs till well incorporated. Add in lime juice & pinch of salt.
5. Pour mixture over baked crust.
6. Bake for an hour & permit to cool. Refrigerate before serving.

Chocolate snickers cheesecake

Yield 12

What you need
3 tbsp butter, melted
1 1/4 c. Sweet biscuit crumbs
1 tbsp white sugar
26oz cream cheese
3 eggs
3/4 c. White sugar
2 tsp vanilla essence
2 snickers bars, chopped

What to do
1. Heat up oven to 355 °f.
2. Mix together melted butter, biscuit crumbs & 1 tbsp sugar. Press to the bottom of a 9 in. Pan. Bake for 10 min..
3. Cream sugar & cream cheese till smooth. Add eggs one at a time, followed by vanilla. Add in chopped snickers bars.
4. Pour mixture right into crust.
5. Bake for an hour. Permit to cool.

Double layer creamy pumpkin cheesecake

Yield 12

What you need

16oz cream cheese, softened
1/2 c. White sugar
1/2 tsp vanilla extract
2 eggs
1 prepared graham cracker crust
1/2 c. Pumpkin puree
1/2 tsp ground cinnamon
1 pinch ground cloves
1 pinch ground nutmeg
1/2 c. Frozen whipped topping, thawed

What to do
1. Heat up oven to 350 °f
2. Mix cream cheese, sugar & vanilla. Pour in eggs one at a time. Pour a c. Of the mixture & spread over bottom of the prepared crust. Put to the side.
3. Add pumpkin, cinnamon, cloves & nutmeg to the remaining mixture & mix lightly till smooth. Pour over the first layer of mixture in the crust.
4. Bake for 40 min.. Let it cool.
5. Refrigerate overnight. Garnish with whipped topping before serving.

Caramel macchiato cheesecake

Yield 12

What you need
2 c. Graham cracker crumbs
1/2 c. Butter, melted
2 tbsp white sugar
24oz cream cheese, softened
1 c. White sugar
3 eggs
8oz sour cream
1/4 c. Brewed espresso or strong coffee
2 tsp vanilla extract

Whipped cream
Caramel ice cream topping

What to do
1. Heat up oven to 350 °f.
2. Mix graham cracker crumbs, melted butter, & 2 tbsp of sugar. Press to the bottom of a lightly greased pan.
3. Bake for 8 min.. Permit to cool.
4. Reduce oven temperature to 350 °f.
5. Beat cream cheese in a bowl till fluffy. Slowly add in 1 c. Of sugar whereas still beating.
6. Beat in eggs one at a time & slowly add sour cream, espresso & vanilla. Pour batter right into the crust.
7. Bake for an hour. Permit to cool.
8. Refrigerate before serving. Garnish with whipped cream & top with caramel ice cream.

Vanilla mousse cheesecake

Yield 16

What you need
40 wafers, crushed
3 tbsp butter, melted
32oz cream cheese, softened
1 c. Sugar
4 tsp vanilla
3 eggs
8oz frozen whipped topping, thawed

What to do
1. Heat up oven to 350 °f
2. Mix wafer crumbs & butter. Press to the bottom of a lightly greased 9 in. Pan.
3. Beat cream cheese, 3/4 c. Sugar & 1 tbsp vanilla with mixer till well blended. Add eggs one at a time. Spread over crust.
4. Bake for an hour. Permit to cool.

5. Mix remaining cream cheese, sugar & vanilla till well incorporated.
6. Beat in whipped topping. Spread over cheesecake.
7. Refrigerate.

Red velvet cheesecake cups

Yield 12

What you need
Crust:
10 chocolate sandwich cookies, crushed
2 tbsp butter

Cheesecake:
12oz cream cheese, softened
1 tbsp sour cream
1/2 c. Sugar
3 tbsp unsweetened cocoa powder
1 tsp vanilla extract
4 tsp red food color
1 egg

Whipped cream:
1/2 c. Heavy cream
2 tbsp powdered sugar
1/2 tsp vanilla extract

What to do
1. Heat up oven to 350 °f.
2. Mix crushed cookies & butter.
3. Press a spoonful of cookie mixture to the bottom 12 cupcake liners
4. Bake for 10 min.. Take away from oven & put to the side to cool.
5. Reduce oven temperature to 325 °f.

6. Mix cream cheese, sour cream & sugar till smooth. Add cocoa powder. Add vanilla & red food color, followed by the egg.

7. Pour mixture right into each liner.

8. Bake for 15-18 min..

9. Permit to cool. Refrigerate.

10. Beating whipped cream ingredients together till soft peaks form. Use to garnish cheesecake cups.

Blueberry cheesecake cups

Yield 24

What you need
8oz cream cheese
3/4 c. Sugar
2 tsp lemon zest, finely grated
1 tsp vanilla extract
2 c. Blueberries
24 vanilla wafer cookies

What to do

1. Mix cream cheese, sugar, zest & vanilla in a food processor. Add blueberries to the mixture.

2. Spread blueberry mixture evenly among 24 cupcake liners.

3. Put a vanilla wafer on top of each cup.

4. Cool down in the fridge overnight.

Honey cheese cups

Yield 8

What you need
9oz ricotta cheese
1/3 c. Caster sugar
1/3 c. Honey
4 eggs
1 tsp ground cinnamon
1 lemon zest, finely grated

What to do
1. Heat up oven to 355 ºf.
2. Mix ricotta cheese, sugar & honey till well incorporated.
3. Add eggs one at a time. Add cinnamon & lemon rind.
4. Pour mixture to 8 lightly greased muffin pans.
5. Bake for 25 min.. Permit to cool afterwards.
6. Garnish with extra honey.

Berry cheesecake cups

Yield 12

What you need
16oz strawberries, halved
1/2 c. Plus 2 tbsp sugar
1 tbsp lemon juice
20oz cream cheese
3/4 c. Sugar
1/2 tsp vanilla extract
1/4 c. Sour cream
2 eggs
3 tbsp all-purpose flour

What to do
1. Heat up oven to 350 °f.
2. Mash together half of the strawberries with sugar. Heat the pan & cook for 3 min..

3. Take away pan from heat & pour in the remaining strawberries together with lemon juice. Permit to cool.

4. Beat cream cheese & add sugar. Add in vanilla & sour cream till well incorporated. Add eggs one at a time & mix with flour.

5. Line a muffin tin with muffin cups. Fill each about 3/4 & bake for 15 min.. Permit to cool.

6. Cool down in the fridge till set & garnish each cheese c. With 1 tbsp of strawberry topping.

Mini berry cheese cups

Yield 10

What you need
1 1/2 c. Graham cracker crumbs
1/4 c. Sugar
1/4 c. Butter, melted
24oz cream cheese
14oz condensed milk
3 eggs
2 tsp vanilla
Raspberries

What to do
1. Heat up oven to 300 °f .
2. Line cupcake tin with cupcake papers .
3. Mix crumbs, sugar & butter. Press mixture right into pan lined with 24 cupcake liners.
4. Mix cheese cream cheese till smooth. Slowly add condensed milk, eggs & vanilla. Mix well.
5. Spread mixture evenly between the cupcake liners.
6. Bake for 20 min. & permit to cool. Refrigerate.
7. Garnish with berries.

Blackberry cheese cups

Yield 10

What you need
1 c. Graham cracker crumbs
1/2 c. Sugar
3 egg whites
16oz reduced-fat cream cheese
2 tbsp all-purpose flour
1 tsp lemon zest, grated
1/2 c. Low-fat plain greek yoghurt
1 tbsp vanilla extract
1 egg
2 c. Blackberries
1/2 c. Seedless raspberry preserves

What to do
1. Heat up oven to 325 °f.
2. Mix graham cracker crumbs, 2 tbsp sugar & 1 egg white in a bowl till combined.
3. Press to the bottom of each liner & bake for 5 - 8 min..
4. Blend cream cheese in a bowl till smooth. Add remaining sugar, flour & lemon zest. Pour in yogurt, vanilla, whole egg & remaining 2 egg whites, one at a time.
5. Spread cream cheese mixture evenly among the muffin cups. Bake for 30 min..
6. Permit to cool. Refrigerate.
7. Garnish each cheesecake with blackberries.
8. Mix remaining blackberries, pre yield & 2 tbsp water right into pan. Bring to a boil over medium heat.
9. Mix well till sauce has thickened.
10. Glaze over cheesecakes.

Chocolate cheesecake cups

Yield 15

What you need

1 1/2 c. Chocolate graham cracker crumbs
2 tbsp sugar
6 tbsp butter, melted
16oz cream cheese, softened
1 c. Hot chocolate mix
2 eggs
2 tbsp sour cream
2 tsp vanilla
2 tbsp flour
1 c. Cool whip
1/2 c. Kraft mini marshmallow bits
1/4 c. Colored sprinkles

What to do
1. Heat up oven at 350 °f .
2. Mix together graham cracker crumbs, sugar & butter.
3. Line baking pan with cupcake liners & put to the side.
4. Blend cream cheese & hot chocolate till creamy.
5. Pour in eggs, sour cream, vanilla & flour & blend again till fully combined.
6. Scoop mixture right into the cupcake liners & bake for 22 min..
7. Turn off the oven, open the door & leave the cheesecake inside to cool for a few min. Before refrigerating.
8. Garnish with cool whip, marshmallows & colored sprinkles.

Miniature cherry cheesecakes

Yield 12

What you need
12 vanilla wafers
16 ounces cream cheese, softened
2 eggs
2 tbsp lemon juice
2/3 c. White sugar
21oz cherry pie filling

What to do

1. Heat up oven to 350 °f .
2. Prep muffin tins with 12 paper baking c. Placing a vanilla wafer in each one.
3. Beat cream cheese till fluffy. Add eggs, lemon juice, & sugar & mix till smooth.
4. Spoon 2/3 cream cheese mixture right into each baking cup.
5. Bake for 15 to 17 min. & permit to cool.
6. Garnish with fruit pie filling or whipped cream before serving.

Sundried tomato cheesecake

Yield 24

What you need
Crust:
5 slices whole wheat bread
1/2 c. Fresh parsley, chopped
1/2 tsp salt
1/2 tsp lemon rind, grated
1/2 tsp black pepper
1 tbsp butter
1 tsp extra virgin olive oil
1 garlic clove, minced

Cheesecake:
1 1/4 c. Sun-dried tomatoes, without oil
1 1/4 c. Cottage cheese
1 tbsp lemon juice
1 tbsp all-purpose flour
1/4 tsp salt
32oz cream cheese
2 egg whites

1/4 c. Fresh basil, chopped
1/2 c. Drained canned artichoke hearts, chopped
13oz melba toast rounds

What to do
1. Heat up oven to 350 °f .
2. Prep bottom of a 9-inch pan with parchment.
3. Mix breadcrumbs, parsley, 1/2 tsp salt, rind, & pepper in a medium bowl.
4. Heat butter in a skillet. Add oil & garlic cook for a min. Whereas stirring continuously.
5. Mix butter mixture with breadcrumbs. Stir.
6. Press breadcrumb mixture to the bottom of the pan. Put to the side.
7. Cover sun-dried tomatoes with boiling water for 30 min.. Drain & finely chop.
8. Beat cottage cheese till smooth. Add lemon juice, flour, salt, cream cheese & egg whites. Mix till smooth.
9. Add tomatoes, basil, & artichoke.
10. Pour filling right into pan.
11. Bake for 30 min.. Let cool.
12. Serve with melba toast rounds.

Roasted pepper pesto cheesecake

Yield 24

What you need

Cooking spray
2 tbsp dry breadcrumbs
15oz ricotta cheese
8oz light cream cheese, softened
1/3 c. Parmesan cheese, grated
1/8 tsp salt
Pinch ground red pepper
1 egg
1 1/4 c. Roasted pepper pesto
1 tsp all-purpose flour
8oz sour cream
French bread baguette, sliced diagonally right into 24

24 roasted red bell pepper strips

What to do

1. Heat up oven to 325 °f .
2. Prep 2 9-inch pans with cooking spray. Dash breadcrumbs over the bottoms of pans.
3. Beat ricotta & cream cheese till smooth. Add parmesan cheese, salt, pepper, & egg. Mix well.
4. Pour 3/4 c. Cheese mixture right into each prepared pan. Spread 1/2 c. Roasted pepper pesto over each layer; top each pesto layer with 3/4 c. Cheese mixture.
5. Bake for an hour.
6. Mix 1/4 c. Roasted pepper pesto, flour, & sour cream in a bowl; mix well. Spread half the mixture over each cheesecake. Bake at 325 °f for 10 min..
7. Take away cheesecakes from oven, permit to cool.
8. Cut each cheesecake right into 12 wedges; serve with baguette slices. Garnish with bell pepper strips, if desired.

Feta cheesecake

Yield 8

What you need
Crust:
3oz white breadcrumbs
1 1/2oz parmesan, finely grated
1oz butter, melted
Black pepper

Cheesecake:
8oz feta cheese
8oz curd cheese
6oz fromage frais
4 heaped tbsp fresh chives, chopped
3 spring onions, finely sliced

2 tbsp lemon juice
2 tsp gelatin
2 egg whites
Black pepper

What to do
1. Heat up oven to 400 °f .
2. Mix breadcrumbs, cheese, melted butter & pepper. Press to the bottom of a lightly greased 9 in. Pan.

3. Bake for 15 min..

4. Process feta cheese, curd cheese & fromage frais till smooth.

5. Add chives, spring onions & pepper.
6. Pour lemon juice & 2fl ounces   water right into saucepan. Dash in the gelatin. Mix to dissolve.

7. In a separate bowl, beat the egg whites till soft-peaks. Heat gelatin mixture to boiling point & add to the cheese.

8. Mix quickly till well incorporated.

9. Steadily add whisked egg whites.
10. Pour the batter onto the crust.

11. Refrigerate cheesecake overnight.

Garlic mushroom cheesecake

Yield 12

What you need
2 tbsp oil
8oz mushrooms, chopped
2 cloves garlic, minced
8.8oz cream cheese, softened

1/2 c. Sour cream
1/4 tsp cayenne pepper
3 eggs
1 tbsp rosemary leaves, finely chopped

What to do
1. Heat up oven to 325 °f .
2. Heat oil in big nonstick skillet. Add mushrooms & garlic. Cook & mix 5 min. Or till softened. Drain.
3. Mix cream cheese, sour cream & cayenne pepper in a bowl till well incorporated.
4. Add eggs, one at a time; mix well. Add in mushroom mixture & rosemary.
5. Pour right into lightly greased 9 in. Pan.
6. Bake for 30 to 35 min.. Permit to cool.
7. Refrigerate overnight.

Double cheese bacon cheesecake

Yield 8

What you need
5oz crackers, crushed
3oz butter, melted
6 rashers bacon, finely chopped
1 onion, finely chopped
18oz ricotta cheese
18oz cream cheese, chopped
1 1/4 c. Parmesan cheese, grated
4 eggs

What to do
1. Heat up oven to 325 °f .
2. Mix crackers & butter. Press to the bottom of a lightly greased 9 in. Pan.
3. Refrigerate crust.
4. Fry bacon & onion in a pan. Put to the side to cool.
5. Mix ricotta, cream cheese, 1 c. Of parmesan, eggs, & salt & pepper till smooth. Add bacon mixture.
6. Pour filling over crust. Garnish with remaining parmesan.

7. Bake for 45 min.. Serve at room temperature.

Vanilla layered cheesecake

Yield 16

What you need
24oz cream cheese
4 eggs
1 1/4 c. Sugar
2 tsp pure vanilla extract
1 ginger graham cracker crust
1 c. Sour cream

What to do
1. Heat up oven to 325° f .
2. Beat cream cheese till smooth. Add eggs one at a time. Add 1 c. Of sugar, 1 tsp of vanilla & mix well.
3, pour batter right into the prebaked crust. Bake for an hour.
4. In a separate bowl, mix sour cream & remaining sugar & vanilla. Pour over crust.
5. Bake again for 5 min.. Permit to cool & cool down in the fridge before serving.

Raspberry cheesecake

Yield 10

What you need
1 c. Gingersnap cookies, crushed
1/3 c. Uncooked quick-cooking oats
2 tbsp butter, melted
Cooking spray
24oz cottage cheese
8 ounces cream cheese
1 c. Sugar

1/3 c. All-purpose flour
1 tbsp lemon rind, grated
1/4 c. Lemon juice
3 big eggs
1 egg white
1 tsp vanilla extract
2 c. Raspberries

What to do
1. Heat up oven to 350 °f .
2. Blend crushed gingersnaps, oats, & butter. Press to the bottom of a lightly greased 9 in. Pan.
3. Bake for 6 min.. Take away & permit to cool.
4. Reduce oven temperature to 325 °f .
5. Mix cottage cheese & cream cheese till smooth. Add sugar, flour, lemon rind, lemon juice, eggs, egg white & vanilla.
6. Pour batter over crust.
7. Bake for one hour & permit cheesecake to cool. Refrigerate before serving.
8. Garnish with raspberries.

Vanilla cinnamon cheesecake

Yield 12

What you need
Crust:
1 1/2 c. Graham cracker crumbs
1/4 tsp ground cinnamon
1/3 c. Butter, melted

Filling:
32 ounces   cream cheese, softened
1 1/4 c. Sugar
1/2 c. Sour cream
2 tsp vanilla extract
1 tsp
5 big eggs

Topping:
1/2 c. Sour cream
2 tsp sugar
1/4 tsp cinnamon

What to do
1. Heat up oven to 475 °f.
2. Mix crust ingredients. Press to the bottom of a lightly greased 9 in. Pan. Put to the side.
3. Beat cream cheese, sugar, sour cream, vanilla & cinnamon till smooth. Whisk eggs & add to the mixture.
4. Pour filling over crust. Bake for 12 min..
5. Reduce oven temperature to 350 °f. Bake for an hour.
6. Permit cheesecake to cool afterwards.
7. Mix topping ingredients & spread evenly over cheesecake. Refrigerate.

Double berry cheesecake

Yield 12

What you need
Crust:
2 c. Graham cracker crumbs
1/4 c. Butter, melted
2 tbsp sugar
1/2 tsp ground cinnamon
Cooking spray

Cheesecake:
24oz cream cheese
1 c. Sugar
1 c. Sour cream
2 tsp lemon rind, grated
1 tsp vanilla extract
3 eggs

Topping:

3/4 c. Blueberries
3/4 c. Strawberries, sliced
2 tbsp sugar
1 tbsp lemon rind, grated
3 tbsp lemon juice

What to do
Crust:
1. Heat up oven to 325 °f .
2. Mix crumbs, melted butter, sugar, & cinnamon in a bowl.
3. Press crust mixture to the bottom of a lightly greased 9 in. Pan.
4. Bake for 10 min.. Permit to cool.

Filling:
1. Beat cream cheese till smooth. Add sugar, sour cream, lemon rind & vanilla. Add eggs, one at a time & mix well.
2. Pour filling over crust. Put pan in a big roasting pan half filled with hot water.
3. Bake for an hour & 20 min.. Permit to cool & refrigerate overnight.

Topping:
Mix berries, sugar, lemon rind & lemon juice. Spread over cheesecake.

Double-chocomalt cheesecake

Yield 10

What you need
7oz malted milk
4oz biscuits, crushed to crumbs
4oz butter, melted
5 tbsp caster sugar
21oz cream cheese
10fl ounces   heavy cream
10oz white chocolate, melted
7oz milk chocolate, melted
2 tbsp malt powder
2oz white maltesers

What to do
1. Mix biscuits, melted butter, 2 tbsp sugar. Press to the bottom of a lightly greased 9 in. Pan & cool down .

2. Divide cream cheese & cream between two bowls, evenly. Add white chocolate to one & milk chocolate, malt & remaining 3 tbsp sugar to an additional. Mix well till smooth.

4. Scoop the milk chocolate mixture evenly right into the pan. Pour the white chocolate mixture over the surface.

5. Garnish with maltesers & cool down overnight.

Creamy lemon cheesecake

Yield 8

What you need
3oz digestive biscuits
2oz butter, melted
7oz cream cheese
18oz fromage frais
7oz confectioners' sugar
5 lemons
4 gelatine sheets

What to do
1. Mix crushed digestive biscuits with melted butter. Press to the bottom of a lightly greased 9 in. Pan. Cool down .

2. Beat cream cheese with fromage frais & confectioners' sugar. Add zest of 2 lemons.

3. Dip gelatine sheets in cold water. Add the juice of 3 lemons & heat over low heat till gelatine is melted. Add right into cheese mixture.

4. Scoop over the crust. Refrigerate before serving.

Melted marshmallow cheesecake

Yield 12

What you need
Crust:
2 1/2 c. Graham crackers crumbs
1/2 c. Granulated sugar
3/4 c. Butter, melted
2 c. Mini marshmallows
1/2 c. Warmed hot fudge ice cream topping

Cheesecake:
16oz cream cheese
1 can sweetened condensed milk
2 tsp vanilla
3 eggs, room temperature
1 c. Mini chocolate chips
2 1/2 c. Mini marshmallows

Topping:
2 chocolate bars, broken right into pieces
1/4 c. Graham cracker crumbs
1/4 c. Warmed hot fudge ice cream topping

What to do
1. Heat up oven to 325 °f .
2. Mix together graham cracker crumbs, granulated sugar & melted butter. Press to the bottom of a lightly greased 10 in. Pan.
3. Arrange 2 c. Of marshmallows over crust & pour hot fudge sauce over marshmallows. Put to the side.
4. For the cheesecake, mix cream cheese, sweetened condensed milk till smooth. Beat eggs one at a time, stirring well. Add vanilla.
5. Add chocolate chips & 2 1/2 c. Mini marshmallows. Spread over crust.
6. Bake for 45 min.. Take away & add remaining marshmallows. Put back in the oven for 5 min..
7. Permit cheesecake to cool. Refrigerate overnight.
8. Garnish with graham crumbs, crumbled chocolate bars & extra hot fudge sauce.

Caramel apple cheesecake
yield 12

What you need
2 tbsp butter
1 c. Brown sugar,
4 apples, peeled, cored, sliced
6oz caramels
1/2 c. Half & half
8oz cream cheese, softened
1/2 tsp pumpkin pie spice
1 1/2 tsp vanilla
1 egg
1/2 c. Milk chocolate chips, chopped
1 pie crust, baked
Pumpkin pie spice
Whipped cream

1. Heat up oven to 375 °f .
2. Melt butter & 1/2 c. Brown sugar in a skillet over medium heat. Mix continuously.
3. Add apples & continue stirring for 15 min. Till apple looks caramelized. Put to the side.
4. In an additional saucepan on low heat, melt caramels in halves till smooth. Keep stirring.
5. Mix cream cheese & 1/2 c. Sugar. Add 1/2 tsp pumpkin spice, vanilla & egg. Mix till well incorporated.
6. Add half of the caramel mixture to the cream cheese batter. Mix apple mixture to the remaining caramel & mix well.
7. Take out apple caramel filling & pour right into crust. Spread chocolate over the filling.
8. Layer it with the caramel cream cheese mixture.
9. Bake for 45 min.. Turn off the oven, open the door & leave the cheesecake inside to cool.
10. Cool down in the fridge till cold. Add pumpkin pie spice right into whipped topping & use to garnish the pie. Return to fridge.

Butter-nutty cheesecake
yield 8

What you need

1 c. Ground vanilla wafers
2 tbsp granulated sugar
2 tbsp butter
1/8 tsp salt
8oz cream cheese, softened
1/4 c. Peanut butter
1/2 c. Sugar
1 egg
2 tbsp heavy cream
1/8 tsp salt
4 fun size butterfinger candy bars, crushed
1 c. Semi-sweet chocolate chips
2-3 tbsp heavy cream
2 fun size butterfingers, crushed

What to do
1. Heat up oven to 350 °f.
2. Mix cookie crumbs, sugar, butter & salt. Press it to the bottom of a lightly greased pan. Bake for 10 min. Next which remove.
3. Reduce heat to 300 °f. Mix cream cheese & peanut butter till smooth.
4. Mix sugar, egg, cream & salt till well incorporated.
5. Add crushed butterfingers. Spread batter over crust.
6. Bake for 22 min.. Turn off the oven, open the door & leave the cheesecake inside to cool for 2 hours
7. Melt chocolate chips. Add cream & mix till smooth.
8. Garnish cheesecake with chocolate mixture.

Lemon berry cheesecake

Yield 8

What you need
3 tbsp butter, softened
1 c. Sour cream
1 c. Graham cracker crumbs
1/4 c. All-purpose flour
32oz cream cheese

1 tbsp vanilla extract
1 1/2 c. Sugar
3 c. Blackberries
3/4 c. Milk
Zest & juice of 1 lemon
4 eggs

What to do
1. Heat up the oven to 350 °f.
2. Mix graham cracker crumbs with butter. Press to the bottom of a lightly greased 9 in. Pan.
3. Beat cream cheese & sugar till smooth. Add milk. Add eggs one at a time till well incorporated.
4. Add sour cream, flour & vanilla. Pour mixture right into two separate bowls.
5. Purée blackberries, lemon zest & juice. Add it to the cream cheese mixture & blend thoroughly.
6. Pour blackberry filling right into the crust. Bake it for 10 min..
7. Take away from oven & add the remaining filling. Return to oven & bake for an hour.
8. Refrigerate before serving.

Chocolate oreo cheesecake

Yield 12

What you need
Cheesecake
16oz cream cheese, softened
2/3 c. Sugar
3 big eggs
1/2 tsp vanilla
1 c. Chocolate chips
1 oreo pie crust

Topping

3 tbsp sugar
8oz sour cream
1 tsp vanilla

What to do
1. Heat up oven to 350 °f .
2. Mix cream cheese, 2/3 c. Sugar, eggs, & 1/2 tsp vanilla till smooth. Pour in chocolate chips & stir. Pour batter right into oreo crust.
3. Bake for 30 min.. Take away from oven & permit to cool.
4. Mix 3 tbsp sugar, sour cream, & 1 tsp vanilla. Pour over warm cheesecake & return to oven for 5 min..
5. Permit to cool & cool down in the fridge before serving.

Nutella cheesecake

Yield 12

What you need
10oz graham crackers, digestive biscuits
5 tbsp butter
13oz nutella
3/4 c. Toasted hazelnuts, chopped
16oz cream cheese
1/2 c. Confectioners' sugar, sifted

What to do
1. Mix finely ground graham crackers butter & 1 tbsp of nutella. Add 3 tbsp of the hazelnuts & continue to blend.
2. Press mixture to the bottom of a lightly greased 9 in. Pan. Refrigerate.
3. Mix the cream cheese & confectioners' sugar till smooth. Add remaining nutella to the cream cheese mixture. Mix well.
4. Pour batter right into crust & spread remaining chopped hazelnuts on top.
5. Refrigerate overnight before serving.

Smoked salmon cheesecake

Yield 15

What you need
Crust:
1/4 c. Breadcrumbs
2/3 c. Parmesan cheese, grated
2 tbsp butter, melted

Cheesecake:
16oz cream cheese, cubed
2 eggs
2 tbsp chives, chopped
2 tbsp parsley, chopped
1 tsp lemon zest
1/4 tsp salt
Ground black pepper to taste
1/2 c. Sour cream
6oz smoked salmon, chopped fine

Garnish:
Chives
Extra breadcrumbs

What to do
Crust:
1. Heat up oven to 350 °f.
2. Mix breadcrumbs, parmesan & butter in a bowl. Press mixture right into the bottom of a 9 in. Lightly greased pan. Put to the side.
3. Beat cream cheese till light & fluffy. Add eggs one at a time; beat well.
4. Mix in chives, parsley, zest, salt & pepper. Add sour cream by hand & chopped salmon.
5. Pour mixture over crust. Put pan in a larger pan filled with 1-inch hot water.
6. Bake for 30 to 40 min.. Permit to cool.
7. Refrigerate overnight.
8. Garnish with chives & breadcrumbs.

Ricotta asparagus cheesecake with swiss almond crust

Yield 8

What you need
2 c. Ground almonds
1 c. Cheese, grated
1/4 c. Butter, melted
2 c. Asparagus, chopped
1/2 c. Arugula, chopped
2 tbsp butter
Salt to taste
4oz cream cheese, softened
2 c. Ricotta cheese
4 eggs
1/4 c. All-purpose flour
1/4 c. Parsley, finely chopped

What to do
1. Heat up oven to 275 °f
2. Mix almonds, grated cheese & butter.
3. Press 1 1/2 c. Of the mixture to the bottom of a lightly greased 10 in. Pan. Reserve the remaining for the topping.
4. Bake for 15 min.. Put to the side to cool.
5. Turn oven temperature to 400 °f .
6. Sauté asparagus & arugula in butter for 10 min.. Permit to cool.
7. Puree cream cheese, ricotta, & eggs till smooth. Add flour & mix till smooth. Add salt & freshly ground black pepper to taste. Mix well.
8. Mix cheese mixture, parsley, & asparagus mixture. Pour over crust.
9. Bake for 15 min..
10. Reduce heat to 375 °f add the remaining of the almond-mixture onto the cheesecake & bake for 35-40 min..

Triple cheese & basil cheesecake

Yield 12

What you need

    Crust:
1/3 c. Parmesan cheese, grated
1/3 c. Panko breadcrumbs
1 tbsp butter, melted
pinch of salt

    Cheesecake:
8oz cream cheese, softened
1/4 c. Feta cheese
1/4 c. Sour cream
2 eggs
1/2 c. Basil
1 tbsp olive oil
1/2 tsp salt

What to do

1. Heat up oven to 350 °f

2. Mix together cheese, bread crumbs, & salt. Press right into the bottom of a 7 in. Springform pan. Put to the side.

3. Put basil in boiling water till leaves are bright green.

4. Transfer to an ice water bath to halt the cooking. Drain & process with olive oil & salt till smooth.

5. Beat together cream cheese & feta cheese till smooth. Beat in eggs, one at a time. Add sour cream & basil mixture & mix well.

6. Pour mixture over crust.

7. Bake for an hour. Permit to cool.

8. Refrigerate overnight.

Creamy leek cheesecake

Yield 12

What you need
16oz cream cheese
2 eggs
1 egg yolk
3 tbsp sour cream
3 tbsp heavy cream
1/4 c. Sautéed leeks, white part only
3/4 c. Cheese, grated
Salt & pepper

What to do
1. Heat up oven to 350 °f .
2. Mix all ingredients together till smooth.
3. Pour the cheesecake batter over a 9 in. Lightly greased pan.
4. Bake for an hour. Permit to cool.
5. Refrigerate.

Pecan & olive cheesecake squares

Yield 12

What you need
1 1/4 c. Breadcrumbs
1/2 c. Pecans, finely chopped
1/3 c. Butter, melted
11oz cream cheese, softened
8oz sour cream
1 tbsp all-purpose flour
1/4 tsp salt

1/4 tsp pepper
1 egg
1 egg yolk
1/2 c. Kalamata olives, pitted, sliced
1 tbsp rosemary, chopped
Fresh rosemary sprigs
Kalamata olives

What to do
1. Heat up oven to 350 °f .
2. Mix together breadcrumbs, pecans & butter.. Press to the bottom of a lightly greased 9 in. Pan. Bake for 12 min.. Put to the side to cool.
3. Mix cream cheese, sour cream, & flour. Add egg & egg yolk, one at a time.
4. Mix in sliced olives & chopped rosemary. Pour mixture right into crust.
5. Bake for 20 min. Or till done. Permit to cool.

Blue cheese & garlic cheesecake

Yield 8

What you need
Cooking spray
16oz cream cheese, softened
1/2 c. Sour cream
4oz blue cheese, crumbled
1 tbsp all-purpose flour
1/2 tsp dried parsley flakes
1/2 tsp dried marjoram
1/4 tsp granulated garlic
2 eggs

Preparation
1. Heat up oven to 325 °f .
2. Mix together cream cheese, sour cream, blue cheese, flour, parsley, marjoram & garlic.
3. Beat in eggs, one at a time. Scoop cream cheese mixture right into 12 baking cups.
4. Bake for 40 min.. Permit to cool.
5. Refrigerate.

Mexican cheesecake

Yield 12

What you need
6 corn tortillas
3 tbsp butter, melted
12oz feta cheese
12oz cream cheese
1 1/4 c. Sour cream
2 cloves garlic, minced
2 jalapenos, finely minced
1 c. Salsa
3 tbsp tomato paste
1 1/4 tsp salt
1 tsp pepper
4 eggs
1/2 c. Cilantro, chopped
2 egg whites, beaten
Watercress
Sliced avocado

What to do
1. Bake the tortillas at 200 °f for 45 min. Or till crisp.
2. Permit to cool & grind in a food processor. Put to the side. Increase oven temperature to 350 °f.
3. Press tortilla crumbs to the bottom of a lightly greased 9 in. Pan.
4. Beat cheeses, sour cream, garlic, jalapenos, salsa, tomato paste, salt, pepper & eggs till smooth.
5. Add cilantro & beaten egg whites.
6. Pour right into prepared pan & dash remaining tortilla crumbs over the top.
7. Bake for 70 min..
8. Turn off the oven, open the door & leave the cheesecake inside to cool for 3-4 hours.
9. Garnish with watercress.
10. Top with sliced avocado. Cut right into wedges & serve with tomato salsa.

Savory vegetable cheesecake

Yield 8

What you need
1 c. Breadcrumbs
2 tbsp nuts, finely chopped
3 tbsp olive oil
16oz cream cheese
1/2 c. Parmesan cheese, grated
1/4 c. Heavy cream
1 egg
Baby spinach
1 artichoke heart
2 green onions, finely chopped
2 tsp dill
1 tsp black pepper

What to do
1. Heat up oven to 325 °f .
2. Mix breadcrumbs, nuts & olive oil till well incorporated. Press to the bottom of a lightly greased 9 in. Pan.
3. Blend together cream cheese, parmesan cheese, heavy cream & egg.
4. Mix in spinach, artichoke hearts, pepper & dill. Add green onions.
5. Pour over crust. Bake for an hour.

6. Refrigerate before serving.

Chicken cranberry-orange cheesecake

Yield 10

What you need
16oz cream cheese
8oz french onion dip
1 tbsp flour
1/2 tsp dill, dried
3 eggs
1 c. Chicken, cooked, minced
1/2 c. Cranberry-orange relish, drained
2 tbsp walnuts, chopped, toasted

What to do
1. Heat up oven to 300 °f.
2. Beat cream cheese till fluffy. Add in onion dip, flour & dill.
3. Add eggs, one at a time, till well incorporated.
4. Add chicken & spread evenly in pan.
5. Bake for an hour. Permit to cool.
6. Refrigerate overnight.
7. Spread relish onto top of cheesecake & dash with walnuts.

Polenta pepper cheesecake

Yield 10

What you need
8 tbsp instant polenta

8 tbsp water
14oz cream cheese
36oz cheese, grated
4 eggs
4.2fl ounces sour cream
8 sweet piquanté peppers
Handful coriander, chopped

What to do
1. Heat up oven to 390 °f
2. Mix water & polenta together. Press to the bottom of a 9 in. Tin.
3. Mix together remaining ingredients. Pour batter right into tin.
4. Bake for an hour.
5. Permit to cool.

Blueberry cabernet cheesecake

Yield 8

What you need
1 pint of blueberries
1/2 c. Cabernet sauvignon
1/2 c. Sugar dissolved in 1/2 c. Boiling water
1/4 c. Heavy cream
1/4 c. Cream cheese
4 tbsp of sugar
1/4 c. Graham cracker crumbs

What to do
1. Puree blueberries, wine & sugar water. Put to the side.
2. Beat cream cheese till light & fluffy. Put to the side.
3. Beat cream & sugar till soft peaks form.
4. Fold cream cheese right into cream & sugar.
5. Put 1/4 c. Of mixture right into a bowl & whisk in graham cracker crumbs.
6. Right into small bowls or popsicle molds, pour 2 tbsp of blueberry mixture. Spread a tbsp of cheesecake mixture on top of blueberry layer. Spread a tsp, of graham cracker mixture on top of cheesecake mixture. Continue layering till top of bowl or mold is reached.

7. Freeze.

Amaretto cheesecake

Yield 12

What you need
Cake:
Cooking spray
1 c. Almonds, finely ground
1/4 c. All-purpose flour
1 tbsp sugar
3 tbsp butter, melted
24oz cream cheese, softened
1 can sweetened condensed milk
2 tbsp amaretto
1 tsp vanilla extract
3 eggs

Brittle:
3/4 c. Almonds, sliced
1 c. Sugar
2 tbsp water
Dash of salt

What to do
1. Heat up oven to 350 °f .
2. Mix almonds, flour, & sugar. Add butter till mixed well.
3. Press mixture to the bottom of a lightly greased 9 in. Pan.
4. Bake for 15 min.. Permit to cool. Reduce oven heat to 300 °f .
5. Beat cream cheese in a bowl till light & fluffy. Add condensed milk, amaretto, & vanilla to mixture & beat till smooth.
6. Beat in eggs, one at a time, beating well next each addition. Pour batter over crust. Bake for an hour. Permit to cool
7. Refrigerate cheesecake.
8. To make brittle, increase oven heat to 350 °f .
9. Put almonds on a baking sheet stirring twice.

10. When cool, put almonds close together in a circle.
11. Heat a saucepan over heat; add sugar, water, & salt to pan. Mix to dissolve.
12. Increase heat & bring mixture to a boil. Boil, without stirring, till caramel is a dark amber color, next which swirl the pan to even out the color.
13. Pour caramel in a circular motion over almonds.
14. Permit brittle to cool & harden. Crush brittle with a rolling pin.
15. Press remaining praline pieces right into top of cake.

Double chocolate liqueur cheesecake

Yield 12

What you need
2oz butter
8oz chocolate
Digestive biscuits, crushed
8oz dark chocolate
14oz cream cheese
4oz caster sugar
4 eggs
9.5fl ounces   heavy cream
5 tbsp kahlúa
6.7fl ounces   crème fraîche
2 tbsp kahlúa
Cocoa powder, for dusting
Extra kahlúa to serve

What to do
1. Heat up oven to 320 °f .
2. Mix together melted butter & crushed biscuits. Press to the bottom of a lightly greased 9 in. Pan. Refrigerate.
3. Melt chocolate over a pan of simmering water whereas stirring. Take away bowl from pan.
4. Mix cheese & sugar till smooth. Beat in eggs one at a time. Add the melted chocolate, cream & 5 tbsp kahluà.
5. Pour mixture over crust & bake for an hour.
6. Refrigerate overnight.

7. Mix crème fraîche & remaining kahluà. Spread over the cheesecake.
8. Garnish with cocoa powder dusting. Serve.

White chocolate frangelico cheesecake

Yield 12

What you need
Crust:
One package chocolate wafers, crumbed
4oz butter, melted

Cheesecake:
24oz cream cheese
3/4 c. Sugar
8oz white chocolate, chopped & melted
1 tsp vanilla
3 tbsp frangelico
4 eggs

What to do
Heat up oven to 350 °f .
Mix together cookie crumbs & melted butter.
Press firmly right into a 9 in. Pan.
Bake 10 min..
Decrease oven temperature to 325 °f .
Beat cream cheese on low for 1 min. Next which slowly add sugar.
Add melted chocolate, vanilla & frangelico & mix only till combined.
Mix in eggs, one at a time, till only incorporated.
Pour filling right into base.
Place pan right into a larger pan half filled with water & bake 60 min. Or till set.
Allow to cool next which refrigerate.

Cheesecake icecream

Yield 16

What you need
1 quart low-fat 1% milk
16oz reduced fat cream cheese, softened
1 1/2 c. White sugar
1/3 c. Triple sec
1 tbsp vanilla extract
1 pinch salt

What to do
Blend all ingredients together & either use your icecream maker as per manufacturer's instructions, or put in freezer, stirring vigorously every 30 min..

Pecan liqueur cheesecake

Yield 12

What you need
2 c. Graham cracker crumbs
1/2 c. White sugar
1 tsp ground cinnamon
1/2 c. Butter, melted
24oz cream cheese, softened
1 1/4 c. White sugar
3 eggs
1/2 tsp vanilla extract
1/2 c. Pecan liqueur
1 c. Sour cream

1/4 c. Confectioners' sugar
1 tsp pecan liqueur
1 c. Ground pecans
1/2 c. Graham cracker crumbs
1 1/2 tbsp white sugar
1/2 tsp ground cinnamon
3/4 c. Pecan halves

What to do
1. Heat up oven to 350 °f .
2. Mix 2 c. Graham cracker crumbs, 1/2 c. White sugar, 1 tsp cinnamon, & melted butter or margarine. Press to the bottom of a lightly greased 10 in. Pan.
3. Beat cream cheese & 1 1/4 c. White sugar. Pour the eggs, one at a time. Mix in vanilla extract & 1/2 c. Liqueur, & blend for 5 min.. Pour the mixture on the crust
4. Bake for 1 hour. Turn off the oven, open the door & leave the cheesecake inside to cool.
5. Blend the sour cream, confectioners' sugar, & 1 tsp liqueur together. Spread over the top of the cooled cheesecake.
6. Mix finely ground pecans, finely ground graham cracker crumbs, 1 1/2 tbsp white sugar, & cinnamon. Garnish cheesecake with pecan mixture.

Cointreau cheesecake

Yield 12

What you need
8oz gingernut cookies
1/2 c. Butter, melted
1/4 c. Cointreau
Pinch of saffron threads
15oz cream cheese
1/2 c. Honey
1 1/2 tbsp orange zest, finely-grated
1 3/4 c. Heavy cream

What to do
1. Blend cookies & butter in a blender till moist & crumbly.

2. Press right into a 9 in. Pan & refrigerate.
3. Heat cointreau in a saucepan till it starts to steam & add saffron threads.
4. Take away from heat & put to the side for 20 min..
5. Beat cream cheese & slowly beat in honey, orange zest & saffron mixture.
6. Continuing to beat, slowly add cream till thick.
7. Spoon the mixture over the base & cool down overnight.

Coffee jelly cheesecake

Yield 10

What you need
Cheesecake:
2 1/2 tsp gelatin, plus 1 tsp
5 tbsp water
6oz shortcake biscuits, crushed
3oz butter, melted
9oz fromage frais
9oz mascarpone
5fl ounces baileys irish cream
4.8fl ounces heavy cream, lightly whipped
2 eggs
5oz caster sugar

Coffee jelly:
1 tsp gelatin
5fl ounces strong black coffee
2 tbsp caster sugar

What to do
Cheesecake:
1. Dash gelatine in water & leave to soak for 5 min.. Put the bowl of gelatine in a pan of lightly simmering water & leave till it appears clear.
2. Mix biscuit crumbs & butter. Press to the bottom of a lightly greased 9 in. Pan.
3. Mix fromage frais, mascarpone & baileys together. Pour in the gelatine & fold in the cream.

4. Beat eggs & sugar in a bowl. Add to the cheesecake mixture & pour onto the crust. Refrigerate for 4 hours.

Coffee jelly:
1. Spoon gelatine over the coffee. Put the bowl in a pan of lightly simmering water till dissolved.
2. Refrigerate the mixture. When cold, prudently pour the coffee mixture on top of the cheesecake to make a thin layer. Refrigerate.

Banana bourbon cheesecake

Yield 10

What you need
2 c. Vanilla wafers crushed
1/2 c. Chopped pecans
4oz butter, melted
3 bananas
1 tbsp lemon juice
1/4 c. Light brown sugar
1 tbsp bourbon whiskey
32oz cream cheese, softened
1 c. Granulated sugar
4 eggs
1 tbsp bourbon whiskey
1/2 c. Vanilla wafers, crushed
1 c. Heavy whipping cream
1/4 c. Powdered sugar
1 tsp bourbon whiskey
1 banana, sliced

What to do
1. Heat up oven to 350 °f .
2. Mix crumbs & pecans in a food processor. Pour in melted butter. Press to the bottom of a lightly greased 9 in. Pan.
3. Bake for 10 min.. Let it cool.

4. Mash the bananas till smooth. Add brown sugar & lemon juice. Heat over a medium heat till the sugar has melted & the bananas cook slightly.

5. Take away from heat & add 1 tbsp bourbon. Blend & let it cool down.

6. Beat cream cheese for 2 min.. Slowly add granulated sugar. Add eggs one at a time, till well incorporated. Add 1 tbsp bourbon.

7. Blend in banana mixture & mix well. Scoop filling over crust & put in a roasting pan half-filled with water.

8. Bake for an hour.

9. In a separate big bowl beat heavy whipping cream. Add powdered sugar & bourbon. Continue whisking till the cream forms soft peaks.

10. Pipe whipped cream onto each slice. Garnish with a vanilla wafer cookie & a banana slice.

Rum-infused mousse cheesecake

Yield 8

What you need
4oz semisweet chocolate, chopped
1 1/2 tsp unflavored gelatin
4 tbsp cold water
8oz cream cheese
1 c. White sugar
2 tbsp rum
2 egg yolks
6fl ounces   heavy cream, whipped
2 egg whites
1 prepared chocolate cookie crumb crust

What to do
1. Dash gelatin over water & permit to soften.

2. In the top of a double boiler, heat chocolate, stirring continously till melted.

3. Put the bowl of gelatin over double boiler & mix till gelatin dissolves.

4. Cream the cream cheese & sugar till light & fluffy. Add rum, egg yolks, dissolved gelatin & melted chocolate.

5. Fold in whipped cream.

6. Whisk egg whites till stiff. Fold right into chocolate mixture.

7. Pour filling right into pie base.
8. Cool down 4 hours or more.

White chocolate cheesecake

Yield 12

What you need
White chocolate cheesecake:
4oz white chocolate
24oz cream cheese
3/4 c. White sugar
1/4 c. All-purpose flour
3 eggs
1/2 c. Heavy cream
1/2 tsp vanilla extract

White chocolate brandy sauce:
2 c. White chocolate, finely chopped
1 c. Heavy cream
2fl ounces brandy

What to do
White chocolate cheesecake:
1. Heat up oven to 300 °f .
2. Cream the cream cheese, sugar, & flour till light & fluffy.
3. Beat in eggs one at a time, mixing well next each addition.
4. Melt 4oz white chocolate and, with mixer on low speed, mix right into cream cheese mixture. Slowly add in the vanilla & 1/2 c. Of heavy cream. Pour filling right into a greased pan.
5. Fill a larger pan 1 to 2 in. Deep with water. Put cheesecake pan right into this pan & bake for 50 to 60 min., or till middle of the cheesecake is only firm.
6. Refrigerate.

White chocolate brandy sauce:

1. Heat 1 c. Heavy cream over a medium-high heat till it boils, next which pour over chopped white chocolate. Mix till melted.

2. Add brandy. Pour over cool down ed cheesecake.

Margarita cheesecakes snacks

Yield 75

What you need
1 can sweetened condensed milk
8oz cream cheese, softened
6oz frozen limeade concentrate
1/4 c. Tequila
2 tbsp triple sec
75 scoop-style tortilla chips
1 c. Heavy whipping cream
2 tsp lime juice
2 tbsp white sugar

What to do
1. Beat together condensed milk & cream cheese till smooth.
2. Add limeade, tequila, & triple sec; & beat till 5 to 8 min..
3. Spoon 1 tbsp cheesecake mixture right into each tortilla chip.
4. Refrigerate till set.
5. Beat cream & lime juice together smooth & thickened.
6. Steadily add sugar till soft peaks form.
7. Top each cheesecake with 1 tsp lime-flavored whipped cream.

Vodka ricotta cheesecake

Yield 8

What you need
Crust:

1 1/4 c. Chocolate chip cookie crumbs
2 tbsp unsalted butter, melted

Filling:
2 pounds ricotta cheese
1 c. Granulated sugar
1/3 c. All-purpose flour
3 big eggs
2 big egg yolks
2 tsp vanilla extract
2 tsp orange zest
1/2 tsp salt

Topping:
1/2 c. Orange marmalade
1/3 c. Vodka

What to do
Crust:
1. Heat up oven to 350 °f .
2. Mix together cookie crumbs & melted butter.
3. Press firmly right into a 9 in. Pan.
4. Bake for 10 to 15 min. Or till done.

Filling:
1. Beat ricotta till smooth.
2. Beat in sugar & flour.
3. Add the eggs & egg yolks one at a time till well incorporated.
4. Blend in vanilla, orange zest, & salt till only incorporated.
5. Pour filling evenly right into base.
6. Bake 1 hour.

Topping:
1. Bring marmalade & vodka to a boil. Reduce to a low heat & simmer till reduced by half.
2. Let stand for 5 min. & pour over cheesecake. Leave 15 min. To set.

Rum praline cheesecake

Yield 12

What you need
1/4 c. Butter
1 c. Graham cracker crumbs
3 tbsp packed brown sugar
1/3 c. Pecans, chopped
16oz cream cheese, softened
1 1/4 c. Brown sugar
3 eggs
1 tsp rum flavored extract
1 tsp vanilla extract
1/4 c. Sour cream
1/3 c. Pecans, chopped
1 1/2 c. Sour cream
1/4 c. Packed brown sugar
3/4 tsp maple flavored extract
1/2 tsp rum flavored extract

What to do
1. Heat up oven to 350 °f.
2. Mix melted butter, graham crumbs, 3 tbsp brown sugar & 1/3 c. Chopped nuts. Press to the bottom of a lightly greased 9 in. Pan.
3. Blend cream cheese & remaining c. Brown sugar till smooth. Add eggs one at a time.
4. Add in 1 tsp rum flavoring, vanilla, 1/4 c. Sour cream & 1/3 c. Chopped nuts.
5. Pour batter over the crust.
6. Bake for an hour & permit to cool.
7. Mix 1 1/2 c. Sour cream, 1/4 c. Brown sugar, maple flavoring, & 1/2 tsp rum flavoring.
8. Spread batter over cheesecake & bake it again for 10 min..
9. Refrigerate before serving.

Pina colada cheesecake

Yield 10

What you need
1 1/4 c. Vanilla wafer crumbs

1 c. Flaked coconut, toasted
1/2 c. Butter, melted
6oz pineapple juice
1 package gelatin
24oz cream cheese, softened
3/4 c. Sugar
1/4 c. Dark jamaican rum*
3/4 tsp coconut extract
2 c. Frozen whipped topping, thawed
20oz crushed pineapple
1 tbsp cornstarch
2 tbsp sugar
Toasted flaked coconut

What to do
1. Mix crumbs, coconut & butter. Press mixture on bottom 9-inch pan. Put to the side in fridge.
2. Pour juice right into saucepan. Dash gelatin over juice & leave to soften.
3. Mix over medium heat till gelatin dissolves. Put to the side.
4. Beat together cream cheese & 3/4 c. Sugar. Beat in gelatin mixture, rum & coconut extract.
5. Fold in whipped topping. Pour filling right into cheesecake base.
6. Refrigerate at least 6 hours.
7. Mix undrained pineapple, cornstarch & 2 tbsp sugar in a saucepan & mix till mixture boils & slightly thickens. Refrigerate.
8. To serve, spoon pineapple mixture over top of cheesecake.
9. Garnish with additional toasted coconut, if desired.

Tiramisu cheesecake

Yield 12

What you need
12oz ladyfingers
4 tbsp butter, melted
4 tbsp coffee liqueur
24oz cream cheese

8oz container mascarpone cheese
1 c. White sugar
2 eggs
4 tbsp all-purpose flour
1oz square semisweet chocolate

What to do
1. Heat up oven to 350 °f .
2. Mix melted butter with finely crushed ladyfingers. Pour 2 tbsp of coffee liqueur & mix well. Press right into the bottom of a 9 in. Pan.
3. Blend cream cheese, mascarpone & sugar till smooth. Pour in 2 tbsp coffee liqueur & mix well. Add eggs one at a time, alternating with flour. Mix slowly till smooth.
4. Pour mixture right into crust.
5. Bake for 45 min.. Leave cheesecake to cool afterwards inside the oven with the door open.
6. Refrigerate next 3 hours. Garnish with grated semi-sweet chocolate.

Rum & chocolate cheesecake

Yield 12

What you need
1 c. Ground almonds
1 c. Whole wheat flour
2/3 c. Vegan margarine
24oz firm tofu
1 1/2 c. Demerara sugar
7 tbsp unsweetened cocoa powder
1/4 c. Sunflower seed oil
1/2 c. Soy milk
1/4 c. Dark rum
1 1/2 tsp vanilla extract

What to do
1. Heat up oven to 325 °f .
2. Mix ground almonds & whole wheat flour. Mix in margarine till a dough is formed. Press to the bottom of a lightly greased 9 in. Pan.

3. Blend together crumbled tofu, sugar, cocoa, oil, soy milk, rum & vanilla till smooth. Spread filling over crust.

    4. Bake for 75 min.. Permit to cool.

    5. Refrigerate before serving.

Vegan cheesecake

Yield 6

What you need
12oz soft tofu
1/2 c. Soy milk
1/2 c. White sugar
1 tbsp vanilla extract
1/4 c. Maple syrup
1 prepared graham cracker crust

What to do
1. Heat up oven to 350 °f .
2. Mix together tofu, soy milk, sugar, vanilla extract & maple syrup. Blend till smooth. Spread over pie crust.
    3. Bake for 30 min.. Let it cool.
    4. Cool down in the fridge before serving.

Tofu cheesecake

Yield 12

What you need
24oz extra firm tofu, drained, cubed
1 c. White sugar

1 tsp vanilla extract
1/4 tsp salt
1/4 c. Vegetable oil
2 tbsp lemon juice
1 prepared graham cracker crust

What to do
1. Heat up oven to 350 °f .
2. Mix together tofu, sugar, vanilla, salt, vegetable oil, & lemon juice. Mix till well incorporated. Spread over pie crust.
3. Bake for 20 to 30 min.. Permit to cool.
4. Cool down in the fridge before serving.

Cashew cheesecake

Yield 12

What you need
2 c. Macadamia nuts
1 1/2 c. Cashews
1/2 c. Dates, pitted
1/4 c. Dried coconut
6 tbsp coconut oil, melted
1/4 c. Lime juice
1/4 c. Raw agave nectar
1/2 sun-dried vanilla bean
3 c. Mixed berries, such as blueberries & raspberries

What to do
1. Put macadamia nuts in a bowl with cold water.
2. Put cashews in an additional bowl with cold water. Soak nuts 4 hours, next which rinse, drain, & put to the side.
3. Crush & blend macadamia nuts & dates in food processor. Spread dried coconut to the bottom of a lightly greased 9 in. Pan. Press macadamia nut batter over the coconut to make crust.
4. Mix cashews, coconut oil, lime juice, agave nectar, & 6 tbsp water in bowl to blend. Take out seeds from vanilla bean & purée till smooth.

5. Pour batter over crust, & refrigerate for an hour.
6. Garnish with berries. Serve.

Strawberry cheesecake

Yield 12

What you need
Crust:
1 c. Almonds
2 tbsp coconut oil, liquefied
3 soft medjool dates
1 tsp pure vanilla extract

Cheesecake
2 c. Raw cashews, presoaked for at least a few hours or overnight
6 tbsp coconut oil, liquefied
Juice of 1 lemon
1 tsp pure vanilla extract
1/4 c. Liquid sweetener of your choice
1 banana
2 c. Strawberries, hulled

Garnish
Extra strawberries for decorating

What to do
1. Mix all crust ingredients. Press to the bottom of 9 in. Pan.
2. Mix all cheesecake ingredients till smooth. Pour mixture over crust & spread evenly.
3. Refrigerate cheesecake overnight.
4. Garnish with extra strawberries on top.

Cashew lime cheesecake cups

Yield 12

What you need
Crust:
2 c. Raw walnuts
3 tbsp maple syrup
1 tsp vanilla

Cheesecake:
2 c. Raw cashews
1/2 c. Coconut oil
2 tbsp maple syrup
1/2 c. Key lime juice
Zest of 4-6 key limes

What to do
1. Mix finely ground walnuts, maple syrup & vanilla.
2. Put 2 tsp of walnut mixture right into 12 cupcake liners
3. For the cheesecake, mix finely ground cashews, coconut oil, maple syrup, lime juice & lime zest.
4. Dash with remaining lime zest. Pour mixture evenly between the cupcake liners.
5. Refrigerate before serving.

Dulce de leche cheesecake bars

Yield 12

What you need
1 1/2 c. Rolled oats
1 c. Walnut pieces
1/2 c. Butter, cold chopped
24oz cream cheese, softened
1 c. Sugar
3 eggs

2 tsp vanilla extract
1 can dulce de leche
1 1/4 c. Chocolate chips
1/3 c. Heavy cream

What to do
Crust:
1. Blend oats & walnuts with a food processor till it turns to fine crumbs. Mix with butter till it starts to come together.
2. Press to the bottom of the lightly greased baking pan to form the crust & let it cool down for half an hour in the fridge.

Filling:
1. Heat up the oven at 350 °f.
2. Blend cream cheese, sugar, eggs & vanilla extract in a food processor.
3. Pour 1/2 c. Of dulce de leech right into the filling mixture & blend. Put to the side the remaining half c. Of dulce de leche.
4. Pour filling right into crust & bake for 40 min..
5. Turn off the oven, open the door & leave the cheesecake bars inside to cool for 3-4 hours.
6. Pour the remaining dulce de leche over it when the cheesecake is ready.

Chocolate layer:
1. Mix chocolate chips & heavy cream & heat in the microwave till chocolate only melted
2. Permit it to cool for a few min. Before pouring over the cheesecake.
3. Let it set for a few hours before cutting right into bars.

Lime cheesecake bars

Yield 12

What you need
Crust:
2 c. Graham cracker crumbs
4oz butter, melted

Filling:

16oz cream cheese, softened
1/2 c. Granulated sugar
2 eggs plus 1 egg white
1/2 c. Sour cream
1 tsp vanilla
2 tbsp all-purpose flour
3/4 c. Prepared lime curd
green food coloring
yellow food coloring

Lime curd:
4oz butter, softened
1 c. Sugar
2 eggs
2 egg yolks
1/3 c. Plus 4 tbsp lime juice

What to do
Crust:
1. Heat up oven to 325 °f.
2. Blend graham cracker crumbs & butter to form the crust. Press to the bottom of the lightly greased pan & bake for 5 min.. Put to the side & permit to cool.
3. Mix food coloring right into 3/4 c. Of lime curd. Put to the side.
4. Beat the cream cheese & sugar till smooth.
5. Beat in eggs slowly one at a time & add sour cream, vanilla & flour to blend again.
6. Pour the mixture over the crust but put to the side a c. Of it for later use.
7. Mix the half c. Of the lime curd with remaining mixture & pour over the top of the cheesecake mixture.
8. Bake for 35 min..
9. Turn off the oven, open the door & leave the cheesecake inside to cool before refrigerating.
10. Cut right into bars to serve.

Lime curd:
1. Cream butter & sugar. Add eggs one at a time whereas mixing.
2. Add lime juice & continue blending till it looks curdled.
3. Cook the mixture over medium-heat till smooth.
4. Lightly increase the heat whereas whisking consistently till it thickens.
5. Take away from the heat & put inside a bowl. Cover the lime curd's surface with plastic wrap.

6. Cool down in the fridge.

Coffee cheesecake bars

Yield 12

What you need
2 c. Chocolate cookie crumbs
1/2 c. Butter, melted
2 tbsp heavy whipping cream
2 tsp instant coffee granules
16oz cream cheese
1/2 c. Sugar
3 eggs
1/2 tsp vanilla
1/3 c. Heavy whipping cream
1/2 c. Semi-sweet chocolate chips

What to do
1. Heat up oven to 350 °f .
2. Mix cookie crumbs & melted butter. Press to the bottom of an ungreased 13x9 in. Pan.
3. Blend whipping cream & coffee granules.
4. Beat cream cheese & sugar till smooth. Add coffee mixture, eggs & vanilla.
5. Pour mixture over crust & bake for 25 min..
6. Pour whipping cream mixture in a saucepan to heat & boil for a min.. Take away from heat & add chocolate chips, stirring till melted.
7. Pour over cheesecake & refrigerate.

One more thing...

If you enjoyed this book or found it useful, i'd be very grateful if you'd post a short review on amazon. Your support really does make a difference & i read all the reviews personally so i can get your feedback & make this book even better.